Voices of
CAMP FORREST
IN WORLD WAR II

Voices of CAMP FORREST IN WORLD WAR II

Dr. Elizabeth Taylor

THE
History
PRESS

Published by The History Press
Charleston, SC
www.historypress.com

Front cover, top: The 136th Infantry Band, 33rd Division, under the direction of First Lieutenant Gleason, welcomes incoming troops from the 80th Division. *USAHEC Military Museum*; *bottom*: Troops of the 80th Division arrived at Camp Forrest in 1942 and then were transported to their new home by truck. *USAHEC Military Museum*.
Back cover, left: Soldiers practicing at the Flippo farm enjoyed having young Glenn around. Several soldiers outfitted him in military garb. *Flippo family collection*; *right*: Nurse Miss Grammar standing in front of the Station Hospital sign in 1941. The War Department continually issued calls for more nurses due to shortages. *USAHEC Military Museum*.

First published 2019

Manufactured in the United States

ISBN 9781625859426

Library of Congress Control Number: 2019947297

Notice: The information in this book is true and complete to the best of our knowledge. It is offered without guarantee on the part of the author or The History Press. The author and The History Press disclaim all liability in connection with the use of this book.

CONTENTS

Acknowledgements 7
Introduction 9

1. Remembering Pearl Harbor 19
2. Constructing and Working at a Military Metropolis 31
3. Growing Up in the Midst of War 79
4. Entertaining the Troops 88
5. It's the Military Life for Me 95
6. Wartime Households 123
7. Enemy, Frenemy and Friend: German Prisoners of War 131
8. Aftermath of War 148

Notes 155
Bibliography 165
Index 173
About the Author 175

ACKNOWLEDGEMENTS

The stories in the following chapters came from listening to hundreds of hours of in-person and previously recorded individual interviews, as well as reading letters, postcards, diaries, biographies, newspapers and other written accounts of life at Camp Forrest, Tullahoma and Middle Tennessee during the pre– and post–World War II years. The author is indebted to numerous individuals and organizations who helped bring this project to fruition. I am especially thankful to the following organizations and individuals for their invaluable assistance: Mrs. Marjorie Collier, Dr. Michael Bradley, the Gore Research Center at Middle Tennessee State University, Mr. Alan Gray, Dr. R.B. Rosenburg, the South Jackson Civic Center, Mrs. Joy Taylor, Tennessee State Library and Archives, Tullahoma Fine Arts Center, The History Press and Arcadia Publishing staff and Mrs. Dot Couch Watson. The memories throughout these pages recount a time when every American mobilized to defeat an enemy located on the other side of the world.

In preparing this book for publication, the author and The History Press made every effort to ensure the information throughout it is accurate. However, we acknowledge at the outset the potential for errors, omissions and misspellings. We apologize in advance should any errors persist, and we request that you notify the publisher with the correct information, so we can update the book for subsequent editions.

INTRODUCTION

Although Camp Forrest was on the American homefront, the important role it played to help win World War II should not be underestimated. Situated in Middle Tennessee in the Cumberland Mountains, Camp Forrest was located two miles from Tullahoma. Tullahoma and its citizens have a long history of serving the U.S. military, from roles in the Civil War to the present day, with Arnold Engineering Development Complex. City officials solicited the War Department (today's Department of Defense) as early as 1911 to build a military base and training facility in the area. The War Department eventually granted permission for construction of a facility; however, work did not commence until the mid-1920s. Tullahoma city officials decided that its national and state guard units should use the facility.

Tennessee was one of only a few states in this era to have national and state guard units. By 1926, the facility was completed and called "Camp Peay," in honor of sitting Governor Austin Peay. The facility consisted of over one thousand acres and accommodated more than twenty-five hundred men for annual maneuvers. Camp Peay had sewage amenities, paved streets and over thirty buildings, including mess halls, barracks, warehouses, administrative buildings, a police station and several bathhouses. The first summer encampment took place from July 17 to August 8, 1926, for more than three thousand national and state guardsmen. The city held several dances at the King Hotel for the guardsmen during the two-week training period. The addition of

Two officers from Camp Peay Police Department standing in front of a car. These officers were on duty during peak and off-peak times of the year. *Author's collection.*

upgrades in the ensuing years, such as extra buildings, lighting and a private water supply, helped modernize the facility. Eventually, construction of an airstrip allowed national guard units to train in Tennessee rather than in South Carolina. In addition to its use as the national and state guard facility, Camp Peay also served as temporary housing for refugees from the Great Flood of the Mississippi and Ohio Rivers of 1937 and occasionally as a state law enforcement and FBI training facility.

After war broke out in Europe in September 1939, federal officials feared the United States would soon become unwitting participants in it. By the end of 1941, and in the span of twenty-four hours, life throughout the nation would forever change with the bombing of Pearl Harbor. By noon the following day, December 8, President Franklin Roosevelt had asked Congress to declare war on Japan. Soon thereafter, Germany declared war on the United States. Even before that ill-fated December day, some parts of the nation had begun readying for war. Governor Prentice Cooper began preparing Tennessee for the inevitable in 1937, via programs such as the civilian defense organization Advisory Committee on Preparedness and by sending representatives to Washington to lobby for the construction of defense industries. Tennessee senator Tom Stewart, Tullahoma mayor Don Campbell and other city officials lobbied the War Department to construct a major military reservation in the state. Washington approved a construction project that would significantly expand the Camp Peay footprint in late September 1940.

By year's end of 1940, the U.S. government had appropriated Camp Peay and began acquiring, by either purchase or lease, thousands of surrounding acres. The survey process for the army training and induction base commenced soon thereafter. With U.S. entry into the war in Europe potentially drawing closer, quick expansion of the military installation and training of soldiers on a grand scale before deployment became key factors in many decision-making processes during the acquisition and construction phases. The existing base expanded to approximately eighty-five thousand acres, and construction was underway by mid-October 1940. The area became a boomtown overnight. The town was plagued by a continual lack of lodging; food shortages; the potential for robbery; labor wage disputes; and repeated muddy, frozen and dusty working conditions. The population soared, as approximately twenty-two thousand to twenty-eight thousand laborers flooded the area during the construction phase.

It cost approximately $36 million to build the 1,300 buildings, fifty-five miles of roads and five miles of railroad tracks within the encampment. The buildings included approximately 408 barracks, 158 mess halls, 14 officer mess buildings, 19 guardhouses, 35 warehouses, 22 gas stations, 20 administration buildings, 30 officer quarters buildings, a bakery, an ice plant, an incinerator, a cold-storage building, a laundry, a water and sewage treatment facility, a dental clinic and a two-thousand-patient hospital. The parking areas throughout the cantonment could accommodate up to four thousand vehicles. The army built several rifle and field artillery ranges, as well as an air-training base, William Northern Field; all were located just north of Tullahoma. As the state's third-largest airfield at the time, Northern Field would become a training site for flight crews in B-24s, B-29s and P-39 Airacobras, observation plane pilots and paratroopers. The base also featured one of the first model "Nazi villages," which afforded U.S. Army Rangers an arena in which to practice realistic combat maneuvers and become familiar with Germanic living accommodations. The village was located on the outskirts of the camp.

Camp Forrest employed approximately 12,000 civilians in a variety of sites, including post exchanges; a nine-thousand-square-foot laundry; vehicle, tank and artillery maintenance areas; and an induction center. According to the Tennessee Historical Society, over 250,000 soldiers received their initial army physical exams at Camp Forrest. When not training for war, soldiers had numerous on- and off-base activities to

CAMP FORREST
TENNESSEE

Sat.
Mar 13, 1943
1:00 P.M.

My darling!

Just sitting here in the Courthouse watching two birds ouside building a nest reminds me that spring is coming. Wish we could be doing likewise or you know what I mean.

I expect you are out this afternoon looking for a gown and my all-important shorts. You sure are lucky to be taken in the O.C.S. after what just happened. Of course though that would not constitute a good reason for keeping you out but you can never tell who would use it to do same. One thing sure, you are no longer his daughter, in a sense, but you are Bob Cook's wife and although maybe we are not at the top of the ladder, we can hold our heads up and look anyone in the eye.

Camp Forrest letterhead was available for both official and unofficial (personal) correspondence. Generally, there was a separate letterhead for bases and regiments. *Author's collection.*

All of the barracks at Camp Forrest were white, two-story wood buildings with minimal interior adornments. The only identifying mark on many were building numbers above the door. *Author's collection.*

occupy their time. Some of the more popular on-base activities included watching movies, attending religious services, attending dinners and dances at service clubs, checking out reading material at the library and shopping at one of the numerous post exchanges. Lieutenant Colonel Arthur Ewert managed the base's twenty-eight chaplains, who worked to ensure soldiers' religious as well as welfare and general education needs were met. Catholic services on base held Mass every Sunday morning, and there were dedicated times for confessions. Jewish services took place every Friday evening. Chaplains held two Protestant services each week. Chaplains for each faith had office hours if soldiers needed additional guidance or counseling. Other base recreational features included a nine-hole golf course; a sports arena; archery and gun ranges; and swimming, tennis and bowling facilities. Throughout the base's operation, more than three hundred couples were married in its chapels. In town, there were five United Service Organizations (USO) clubs, three movie theaters, a

Reading hall adjoining the library, which was located in the Service Club, offered an excellent selection of reading materials. *American Library Association Archives.*

bus station, a railroad station, restaurants, a multitude of churches and countless nightclubs and bars. With a day pass, soldiers could take bus or train trips to visit nearby cities, such as Nashville and Chattanooga.

In June 1941, the "Tennessee Maneuvers" began throughout the state, providing soldiers with realistic war experiences. The Middle Tennessee terrain most closely resembled the European front and provided realistic simulations for war-game activities. Residents became accustomed to soldiers camping out on lawns and porches, the continual construction (sometimes de-construction) and the constant maneuvers/training exercises by the various "Red" and "Blue" army forces. General George S. Patton's Second Armored ("Hell on Wheels") division came from Fort Benning, Georgia, to participate in the maneuvers. Property owners often sought reparations from the federal government for damages caused by troops and tanks. In addition to property damage, livestock also were often "victims" of war games. The loud noises, farmers complained, caused hens to stop laying eggs and cows to stop giving milk.

The streets of Tullahoma were continually crowded once construction started and did not end until Camp Forrest was decommissioned. *Author's collection.*

In 1942, Camp Forrest transitioned from primarily a training and induction facility to one dedicated to the detention of individuals regarded as "enemy aliens." The War Department briefly considered sites in Crossville for an enemy alien detention camp. However, the War Department never provided final approval, and Camp Forrest housed the suspected enemy aliens. During a ten-month period, the federal government referred to the facility as "Camp Forrest Enemy Internment Camp." As many as eight hundred individuals along the East Coast and throughout the Southeast whom the government deemed enemy aliens were detained in specially built areas within the cantonment. The government deemed some enemy aliens a threat to national security only because, if returned to their home country, they would be forcibly drafted into the military or possessed a skill that could advance the Axis war effort.[1] By mid-1943, the War Department transferred everyone to Fort Lincoln, North Dakota, and Camp Forrest became a prisoner of war (POW) camp.

It was now referred to as the "Camp Forrest Prisoner of War Camp," and the first POWs arrived there in June 1943. The prisoners consisted of approximately fifteen hundred Germans, as well as hundreds of Italians and a small group of Japanese soldiers. There is very little information regarding the detention of Italian POWs at Camp Forrest. Newspaper accounts seem to indicate that the repatriation of the Italian POWs did not occur immediately upon Italy's surrender. Many stayed in the area and secured work on local farms until they were able to return home.[2] Churches often allowed the men to sleep in classrooms, as there was nowhere else for them to go. Stories from neighboring Camp Crossville denote a bitter hatred between the German and Italian detainees, so the groups were housed in separate compounds on the 194-acre facility. There were several instances of German soldiers pulling the limbs of Italian soldiers through the barbed-wire fences in an attempt to cause serious bodily harm.[3]

The first wave of German POWs to arrive was mainly from Erwin Rommel's Afrika Korps, captured during the North African campaign. By 1944, Camp Forrest detained an average of 20,480 German prisoners. The facility processed and sent prisoners to other POW camps located throughout the United States. Some prisoners were permanently "stationed" at Camp Forrest. During this time, the media did not widely publicize information about the nationality and number of prisoners detained or specifics of the camp. This suppression was at the behest of federal and state governments, which believed that the knowledge would incite fear, panic or outrage if the public knew. Throughout Middle Tennessee, however, people were well aware of the "secret population" housed at Camp Forrest.

During their confinement in Tennessee, POWs served in support roles within and outside of the facility. With the bulk of Tennessee's male population serving in uniform, farmers became desperate for help during the various harvest seasons. Prisoners routinely left the camp under guard to assist with harvesting crops and pulpwood production, unloading boxcars of supplies at train depots and weaving camouflage nets. POW housing consisted of small huts in a specific section of the cantonment. Accounts indicate that these buildings did not have adequate insulation, and rains caused the floors inside the living quarters to be continually muddy.

POWs had access to medical, dental, educational and recreational facilities throughout their detainment. The government instituted the "Intellectual Diversion Program" to educate POWs on appreciating and respecting American culture and its citizens. The Geneva Convention authorized the use of these programs. Attempts to gain the individual's confidence and change mindsets were not considered subversive measures. American officers helped POWs obtain educational and recreational materials to understand the value of democracy. The government eventually replaced education correspondence courses with face-to-face courses taught by local instructors on the base. POWs had access to a variety of courses, such as English language, grammar, U.S. history and geography.

To pass the time, POWs staged theatrical productions, started bands/ orchestras and produced a camp newspaper. Many days throughout the cantonment, Italian POWs sang beautiful arias from their favorite operas. POWs regularly corresponded with family and friends back in Germany and received cards and letters from home. Both American and German postal censors reviewed all correspondence before allowing them to proceed to their destinations. Censors had to ensure documents were free of secret messages or codes. Many POW letter writers declared how much they missed their family, friends and homeland but seemed grateful that they were no longer fighting.

Activities at the prisoner camp drastically reduced after D-day in France in early June 1944. The war ended in late 1945; Germany surrendered on May 8 and Japan on September 1. By August 1945, approximately three thousand sick or wounded ambulatory German POWs at Camp Forrest were shipped back home. Prisoner repatriation halted by the end of the year so returning American GIs could make it home by Christmas. The federal government decommissioned Camp Forrest by 1946, citing high operational costs in maintaining the complex. Eventually, its land, buildings and material goods were all deemed surplus.

Buyers rebuilt many of the purchased buildings, such as chapels and barracks, in new locations. Many of these buildings are still in use throughout the Southeast. In 1951, the area's footprint expanded significantly and became an Air Force Test Center and Air Force Material Command, Arnold Engineering Development Complex (AEDC). The current eighty-five-thousand-acre AEDC complex encompasses the original Camp Forrest footprint and is one of the most globally advanced and largest test-flight simulation facilities. When the war ended, lives and the landscape were irrevocably changed. Today, the only physical reminders of Camp Forrest are a few decaying chimneys, old roadbeds and concrete slabs. Nevertheless, the memories of those who worked at or were stationed at Camp Forrest or who recall its history have survived.

This volume bridges the gap between historical knowledge and personal accounts of individuals in Middle Tennessee in the 1940s, when Camp Forrest was a thriving military installation and POW facility. The oral histories contained within feature perspectives from children and young adults growing up around a large military installation, soldiers who trained there, civilians who worked there and prisoners of war who called it "home" after being captured. Chapter 1 focuses on how individuals in Tullahoma and at Camp Forrest learned about the bombing of Pearl Harbor. The sentiments express their reactions as the United States officially entered the Second World War. Chapter 2 describes life and experiences of building and working at a military "metropolis." Chapter 3 looks at how children and teenagers navigated life and loss amid a global conflict abroad and the simulated ones in their own backyards. Chapter 4 describes the entertainment that residents and soldiers enjoyed during the war years at Camp Forrest and in Tullahoma. Chapter 5 recalls military life experiences from individuals stationed at Camp Forrest. Chapter 6 recounts how Middle Tennessee households adjusted throughout the war; the influx of people to the area; life in the shadow of a major military installation; and the life, loves and marriages that resulted because of Camp Forrest. Chapter 7 describes the prisoner of war experience in the area. Chapter 8 recounts the dramatic postwar effects on Middle Tennessee when Camp Forrest was decommissioned and Arnold Engineering Development Complex (AEDC) became operational.

1

REMEMBERING PEARL HARBOR

lthough the United States remained neutral as the war in Europe continued to escalate in the late 1930s, the federal government began preparing its infrastructure for when the inevitable happened. Americans were aware of the horrors occurring abroad from daily accounts in national, regional and local newspapers and radio programs. Nevertheless, most citizens strongly opposed engaging in any foreign wars. The overseas fighting, which was eventually dubbed World War II, began on September 1, 1939, with the German invasion of Poland followed by Great Britain's and France's declarations of war on Germany. The first U.S. peacetime military draft started in September 1940. It required male citizens ages eighteen to sixty-four to register for military service. By mid-1941, activation of militias throughout the nation and assessment of war industry production capabilities and general readiness began. President Franklin Roosevelt dubbed the U.S. industrial production efforts as the Allied nations' "Arsenal of Democracy." Radio and newspaper headlines announced that the sleeping giant had fully awakened by Monday morning, December 8, following the surprise attack on Pearl Harbor. Enlistment offices could barely process all of the men ready to sign up to fight the Axis.

Tennessee Prepares for War

It had been only twenty years since "The Great War"—now known as World War I—ended. However, it was still in the forefront of many Americans' minds. In 1937, Tennessee governor Prentice Cooper participated in a Rotary-sponsored tour of Europe. During this trip, he met with Adolf Hitler. The German military preparations for a possible war he witnessed during his trip, as well as his discussions with Hitler, gave him cause for alarm. Governor Cooper foresaw American involvement as imminent in a European war instigated by Hitler. When he returned to Tennessee, he began readying his state for any eventuality. By 1940, Tennessee had established various civilian defense organizations, such as the Advisory Committee on Preparedness.

Washington reports in the days preceding December 7 indicated that negotiations between President Roosevelt and the Japanese ambassador had not yet faltered but had clearly stalled. Reports detailing FDR's personal message to Emperor Hirohito on the evening of December 6 provided Americans hope that this last-ditch effort would resurrect the stalled negotiations with Japanese Premier Hideki Tojo and other diplomatic envoys. The unprovoked attack hours later revealed the futility of FDR's efforts. After learning of the attack, Roosevelt held numerous conferences with cabinet and congressional members at the White House throughout Sunday afternoon.

Over seventy-five years have passed since the original day of infamy—the bombing of Pearl Harbor. Although the direct connections with this aspect of our past are fading, the memories of those who lived through this decade are vivid and preserved for posterity. Tullahoma was more than 4,200 miles from Hawaii, but it still bore witness to the events and tragedy that drew America into World War II.

December 7, from Hawaii to Tennessee

An active U.S. naval base had been located on the largest island of Hawaiian territory for four decades. As Hawaii would not attain statehood until 1959, many Americans were unaware of its location. The attack on Pearl Harbor sank or damaged 18 warships, destroyed 164 aircraft and killed more than twenty-four hundred service members and civilians. Tennesseans with loved ones stationed in Hawaii waited anxiously for reports that they were unharmed. Radio broadcasts provided listeners with breaking coverage for the rest of the day. A KGU reporter in Honolulu provided a live report of the fighting at Pearl Harbor by telephone. Operators disconnected the call to the NBC New York division after two minutes. This call was the only live report of the battle and devastation that had occurred that morning. Correspondents hurriedly submitted stories and eyewitness accounts to editors and the national wire services. Newspapers across the nation published extra editions for their readers detailing the state of the nation. The bombs may have crippled the pride of the Pacific fleet, but they strengthened America's resolve to help destroy the Axis powers.

The December 7, 1941 home edition of *Kingsport Times* in East Tennessee was a typical Sunday paper containing updates on the war, regional and local news, sports stories, the society section and numerous ads detailing sales and Christmas must-haves. Other front-page articles detailed the holiday rush retailers anticipated for Christmas 1941, since economic

JAP PHOTOGRAPH OF RISING SUN PLANE OVER PEARL HARBOR.   US NAVY PHOTO 100-19

Japanese photograph of a rising sun plane flying over Pearl Harbor on the morning of December 7, 1941. *Author's collection.*

projections suggested it would be one of the gayest and happiest in years. Sales had already surpassed the previous year. J.A. Godwin, manager of the local Montgomery Ward, remarked that customers did not seem as price-conscious and purchased items without hesitation. Perhaps the lack of hesitation was due to the monies and jobs now available because of the construction of a city-sized military installation, Camp Forrest. Other military installations were also under construction during this period in Tennessee: Camp Campbell, on the Kentucky border, Camp Tyson, a barrage balloon training camp in Paris, Stewart Air Base, located southeast of Nashville and Oak Ridge.

The editors of the *Kingsport Times* published the first extra edition that Sunday afternoon. The headline took up half of the front page and declared in huge, bold capital letters, "U.S. AT WAR WITH JAPAN." The rest of the front page decried the devastation, chaos and loss of life at Hickam Field (Hawaii's principal army airfield and bomber base), Pearl Harbor and Honolulu. The remaining three pages of the extra edition paper contained reports and statistics of the devastation, a two-page military-related "Picture Parade" section and reprints of articles detailing FDR's attempts to contact the Japanese emperor. The Monday morning edition of the *Tennessean* of Nashville detailed not only the unprovoked attack but also how the 129th and 13th Illinois Infantries and the 107th Ohio Cavalry battalions had already dispersed throughout the state to guard strategic facilities. By Monday afternoon, other state newspapers released extra editions explaining the U.S. declaration of war on Japan and new events that had occurred on the world stage.

THE FIRST OF MANY WARTIME CHRISTMASES

The thermometer was dropping that December 1941, as individuals readied themselves for the holidays—only fifteen shopping days left until Christmas. Throughout the Southeast, "Old Man Winter" made it necessary to wear heavy coats and scarfs. The smells of Christmas filled many grocery stores, as the provisions of spices, nuts and dried fruits packed shelves. "Merry Christmas" banners and decorations ornamented storefront windows; on each lamppost hung a wreath with twinkling lights. Children's eyes lit up as the magic of the toys in the window displays captured their imagination. Homes had trees decked with shiny bright ornaments, tinsel, candy canes and a humble angel on top. The aroma of trees, holiday cakes and cookies filled homes, and wreaths and Christmas cards decorated walls.

Local newspapers contained numerous pages of ads for stores, such as Lockes Five and Dime, Clayton Shoe Store, Rollins & Levan Furniture Store, Dells and Mrs. John Dutton's "Wonder Shop." Stores advertised Christmas gifts of jewelry, women's dresses, men's shirts and ties, furniture, hats, toys and toiletry sets. "Father Christmas" left a myriad of wonderful presents under the tree that year: a new hat for mom, a spiffy tie for dad, a new doll for baby sister and a baseball glove for big brother. However, the best gift that year were the moments spent with family and friends, as the future was now uncertain. War was declared only seventeen days earlier, so America was starting to enter its darkest hours.

The news of the day in the 1940s emanated from only a few sources: newspapers, radios and neighbors. Many residents subscribed to multiple local and regional newspapers and magazines. Popular newspapers included the *Tullahoma Guardian*, the *Tennessean* and the *Chattanooga Times-Free Press*. Popular national magazines included *Life*, *Saturday Evening Post* and *Better Homes and Gardens*. Many 1940s Middle Tennessee residents owned either an electric or a battery-powered radio. Listeners could tune into local and national news programs, as well as be entertained by sporting events, comedy and mystery programs and live music. Citizens tuned in to listen to the evening news and FDR's fireside chats to learn about the state of the nation. Joanne Roberson remembered vividly that she and her siblings were to remain very quiet during the radio news broadcasts.

Amid the flurry of activity in town, many residents listened to the radio for updates on the war. Radio programs that Sunday were continually interrupted as announcers provided updates on the devastation and state of the nation. Since the Japanese had also attacked U.S. forces and Manila in the Philippines, Americans feared that an aerial attack on the mainland was imminent.

In her weekly Sunday evening radio program, *Over Our Coffee Cups*, First Lady Eleanor Roosevelt spoke of the devastation and the state of the nation. She was the first public figure to address the nation since the attack occurred. Her message asked Americans to pull together and do whatever necessary to boost the morale of our service members. Reports of her broadcast described the ever-diplomatic First Lady as speaking calmly and instilling listeners with a sense of confidence as she reminded them they were the "free and unconquerable people of the United States of America." President Roosevelt's congressional address was at 12:30 the next

TULLAHOMA HIGH SCHOOL, TULLAHOMA, TENNESSEE   H-599

Above: Tullahoma High School added three new teachers to accommodate the anticipated increase in student population as new families moved to the area. *Author's collection*.

Left: As the war progressed, posters reminding citizens of the devastation incurred on December 7 ensured that support for the war effort did not wane. *NARA-CP*.

afternoon, December 8. Students in Tullahoma and the neighboring towns filled school auditoriums to listen to the president's message. The mood was somber in most of them, as students and faculty silently listened to the ten-minute address. With the 388–1 congressional vote that followed, our nation was at war. (Jeannette Rankin (R-Montana) was the only member of Congress to oppose the declaration of war.) Many children were too young to understand the depth and meaning of Roosevelt's message. Those teenagers old enough to understand it presumed the war would be over quickly. Many did not realize how many friends and family members would pay the ultimate price for ensuring freedom. By Monday afternoon, the president signed the formal declaration of war. On December 11, Germany and Italy declared war on America. The construction at Camp Forrest may have been silent that Sunday afternoon, but work resumed early the next morning at breakneck speed.

CIVILIANS REMEMBER...

At the Couch home on Atlantic Avenue in Tullahoma, the radio was playing in the living room while the family's oldest son, seventeen-year-old Bob, a sophomore in high school, was completing his homework so he could go see a movie at the Strand Theater that evening. His older sister Searcy[4] and their grandfather Daddy Billy were in the front porch swing when the opera program playing on the radio was interrupted with the news that Pearl Harbor had been attacked. Everyone listened intently to the broadcast as details of the devastation continued to unfold.

James Gist[5] turned seventeen that summer and enjoyed being a Tullahoma High School senior. The Tennessee native was home alone listening to the radio when the news broke in at 5:00 p.m. to alert the public of the attack. He recalled wondering where in the world the devastation occurred. While he learned geography in school, it was uncommon for people to travel beyond their state's borders. This norm caused many citizens to consult an atlas or a neighbor to discern the exact geographic location of the devastation. There was no television to watch to learn more about the current state of affairs. James walked three blocks to the center of town to see what others may have heard about the attack. There were very few people available to talk to when he arrived, as soldiers were scurrying throughout the city trying to get back to Camp Forrest as quickly as possible. Bob Couch[6] was at the movies and recalled that shortly before dark most soldiers in the theater received orders to return to base immediately. Preparations were quickly made for deployment to protect most of Tennessee's strategic civilian areas, such as post offices, fire departments, dams, waterworks, telephone offices, train depots and all other establishments susceptible to espionage and/or sabotage. Gist was surprised when all Tullahoma High School students were required to assemble in the auditorium Monday morning. However, most schools, from elementary to high school, gathered their students into auditoriums to listen to radio broadcasts. After listening to the president's address, it was not until much later that the boys in James's class became fully aware of the gravity of the moment, with their enlistment to fight the Axis powers. Euther Chesser learned about the attack from his stepfather, who left work to tell the family the news. He, too, consulted the family atlas to find the location of Pearl Harbor.[7]

Dorothy "Dot" Morton (later Couch) and her family were visiting an aunt in Chattanooga when they learned of the attack. As she was a young child at the time, the news frightened her. She, like many Americans, was fearful of further attacks on American soil.[8]

Paris Brewer[9] was also seventeen years old but vividly remembered the emotional upheaval his family and friends experienced as conversations and newscasts gradually revealed the details on the loss of life and damage to military resources at Pearl Harbor. Like many others, Brewer did not think the war would last long. Little did he and others know it would be four long years of conflict.

Dlorice Stanaland[10] was studying in her Western Kentucky College dorm room when the news broke on the radio. Everyone in the dorm sat around the radio in hushed silence as news reports continued throughout the afternoon and evening. She eventually left college when a friend helped her attain a secretarial position for the chief of surgical services at Camp Forrest. Federal positions paid more than civilian positions, such as bank clerks and schoolteachers. Many individuals put scholastic pursuits on hold to earn money and support the war effort.

In interviews for the Tullahoma Fine Arts Center's 2001 exhibit Sacrifice and Prosperity: The Tullahoma Experience during World War II, several citizens recalled what they were doing when they heard the news.

Elizabeth Jennings remembered she and her husband, L.B. Jennings, were driving home from church when they heard the news. R. Pierson Smith, a

Tom Vance Lawson and Louise Brown Byck stand by the roadster she drove throughout the war years. *Alan Gray Collection.*

solider stationed at Camp Forrest was at the Maxwell Hotel in Nashville when he heard of the attack. William (Buss) Holt, Sr. was getting off a bus at Twin Oaks when someone came running out of the store shouting "they bombed Pearl Harbor, they bombed Pearl Harbor." Mrs. Anita Kohl was working at the telephone company switchboard when the news broke.

Alan Gray[11] recalled stories of when his cousin Louise Brown Byck, who was visiting from Murfreesboro, became distraught with fear and panic after learning of the bombing. She was visiting her cousins the Lawsons in Tullahoma but immediately jumped into her roadster to leave after hearing the news. She grabbed her cousin's daughter, Shirley, as she left the house. Shirley stood up in the roadster's floorboard as Louise sped home, listening to the news on the radio the whole way. As they reached Murfreesboro, young Shirley wondered why Louise would prefer to listen to the war reports rather than music. It was a mystery why she sped home and took little Shirley with her after learning of the bombing.

Being very young at the time, individuals such as Glenn Flippo (age seven), Mary Ruth Dean (age five) and Johnny Majors (age seven) were aware something occurred but did not fully grasp the changes that were about to unfold around them. Many parents did not discuss the war with very young children for fear of the trauma it might inflict. These youngsters would become more aware of the situation once Camp Forrest was operational and a sea of khakis inundated the area.

SOLDIERS RECALL THE EVENTS...

Lieutenant General Ben Lear, commanding general of the U.S. Second Army from October 1940 to April 1943, noted the positive and negative aspects of the armed forces in a meeting with commissioned personnel at Camp Forrest on December 1. The basis for his remarks was his review of the Red and Blue Army's performance after the Carolina and the Arkansas-Louisiana war-game maneuvers. He felt the losses to American forces on the European front would be "overwhelming" if measures were not taken to ensure troops were proficient in the fundamentals of combat.[12] Training at Camp Forrest intensified that following week by focusing on field maneuvers.

There was nothing out of the ordinary on base that Sunday morning. Many soldiers were enjoying their day off, attending church, preparing for the next week, writing letters home, going into town for entertainment and Christmas shopping, reading or simply relaxing. Some of the soldiers of the Thirty-Third Illinois Division were preparing for the three-day inspection of Camp Forrest's training programs by Major General Robert C. Richardson Jr., VII Army Corps commander. However, inspection plans would change radically by day's end.

Chicago native Harry Pavey[13] did not partake in many of the recreational activities in Tullahoma like his fellow soldiers. He spent his free time visiting his girlfriend and her parents in Nashville. It was during one such visit over dinner that Pavey, his girlfriend, Mildred, and her parents learned of the Pearl Harbor attack. He returned to the base as soon as possible after learning the news.

Wesley Allen Kirby[14] was on guard duty at Post Number 8 in the warehouse area. Although he had a .45 caliber pistol in its holster hanging from his waist, it was unloaded. Being on duty, he had not yet learned the news of the attack until the sergeant of the guard traded the unloaded pistol for a M1 rifle with two clips of ammunition. The sergeant of the guard said, "The orders of the day are to guard this post because Japan just bombed Pearl Harbor." Kirby was to challenge everyone who was on the post that came

In the front are Camp Forrest Headquarters and other administrative buildings. To the far left is the camp post office. *Northwestern University Library*.

into his compound. If they did not challenge back, he was to immediately shoot to kill. Luckily, no one attempted to access his area of the post that day. The prevailing sentiment among the soldiers was that it was war and that everyone should be on high alert. By the first of the year, his division had transferred to the West Coast.

Although his twentieth birthday was still twenty-one days away, a young Illinois guardsman, Richard Koepke,[15] had attained the rank of sergeant. As company duty sergeant, Koepke was required to remain on base that cold December day. That day started peacefully, so he was relaxing and reading the Sunday paper in his quarters. The commotion outside startled him, and personnel began to shout "the Japs had bombed Pearl Harbor!" In disbelief, he presumed the men were referring to another nation being bombed. He reported immediately to his company's senior officer. The lieutenant's orders were to call all soldiers back to base and have them ready as soon as possible to move out to an unknown destination with their full field packs. Amid the chaos, he also ordered men to load machine-gun belts and Browning automatic rifle magazines with ammunition and pack up kitchen equipment. Within hours, several companies shipped out to various destinations throughout the nation. Several troops received orders to help defend the U.S. West Coast from potential attacks. Military personnel and civilians were fearful the Japanese might soon mount additional air attacks on strategic military points along the Pacific. Many in Koepke's division received orders to guard Chattanooga's powerhouses and dams. In answering President Roosevelt's call for building fifty thousand aircraft, Koepke eventually transferred to the air corps. With a call to build that many planes, he knew they would need pilots to fly them.

Camp commanders immediately canceled all leave requests indefinitely due to the continued uncertainty. However, by December 12, local newspapers reported that commanders had a plan allowing soldiers Christmas furloughs. Commanders began approving the furloughs, which were staggered so that each soldier was able to go home for two weeks while the base had adequate members to maintain operations. The Jewish soldiers voted unanimously to forgo their leaves so that more soldiers who were Christian could be home at Christmas. While some did not make it home for Christmas, they were able to ring in the New Year at home. The morale officer for the Illinois Thirty-Third Division, Major H.I. Szymanski, and area residents worked to ensure that the spirts of men remaining at Camp Forrest for the holidays remained high. Soldiers who did not make it home spent their spare time helping to decorate the cantonment, from PXs and lounges to barracks and hospital wards. Regiments and organizations held numerous fun-filled parties in the days leading up to Christmas, in which games and holiday confections added to the gaiety. On Christmas Eve, soldiers and military bands walked company streets caroling and several truckloads of men serenaded residents in town via sound trucks.[16] Various religious services took place on Christmas morning. That evening, soldiers enjoyed a big turkey dinner complete with mashed potatoes, cranberries, plum pudding, mince and pumpkin pie, as well as candy and nuts. In an attempt to ameliorate homesickness throughout the holiday, residents invited soldiers into their homes to enjoy meals and camaraderie.

Even before President Roosevelt asked Congress for a declaration of war, Americans, both young and old, were starting to unite and rally around Old Glory to ensure ultimate victory over the Axis powers. Whether it was helping construct a military metropolis, easing a soldier's homesickness, rolling bandages or giving blood, everyone had a role to play in this new global conflict.

2

CONSTRUCTING AND WORKING
AT A MILITARY METROPOLIS

I need not repeat the figures. The facts speak for themselves....These men could not have been armed and equipped as they are had it not been for the miracle of production here at home. The production which has flowed from the country to all the battlefronts of the world has been due to the efforts of American business, American labor, and American farmers, working together as a patriotic team.
—*President Franklin D. Roosevelt, Navy Day speech, October 27, 1944*

Middle Tennesseans still felt the effects of the Depression when the War Department announced federalization of Camp Peay. Its expansion into a major military induction and training facility could provide the state with much-needed economic relief. The economic downturn caused by the Great Depression forced businesses to lay off workers, reduce wages or permanently close their doors. Families throughout the area were unable to pay property taxes and eventually lost their farms. The hope of work brought people to the Tullahoma area even before the government issued formal employment announcements. Residents fully understood how this federal construction project would help bolster the local economy. Soon after the announcements, local businesses experienced a sharp increase in inquiries and sales. Camp Peay, in addition to possessing a terrain and climate similar to the European front, made Tennessee's Coffee and Franklin Counties logical choices for a major military installation. In preparation for construction, the federal and state governments began acquiring land from local residents and expanded the site's footprint from one thousand to eighty-five thousand acres. Many residents readily sold or leased their property, while others felt the government was undervaluing their property. Many of these individuals were farmers whose protests stemmed from the awareness their compensation would not enable them to secure another farm. Unable to secure the required acreage, the War Department indicated that it would begin looking for comparable sites elsewhere to build the cantonment.[17] State and local officials sprang into action, visiting hundreds of individuals throughout the proposed military installation site in an effort to secure the remaining acreage.

When it was finally completed, the cantonment was one of the largest training and induction facilities in the United States, serving as the training grounds for infantry, artillery, engineering and signal divisions, as well as numerous specialized advanced schools. There were approximately eighty-one different battalions stationed at Camp Forrest at various points throughout the war. The battalions included personnel from the following military units:

Long-Term Assignment[18]
33rd Division
75th Field Artillery Brigade
80th Division
8th Division
17th Airborne Division
5th Armored Division
2nd Ranger Battalion
5th Ranger Battalion

Short-Term Assignment
5th Division
26th Division
78th Division
106th Division
30th Division
79th Division

Unattached Units
257th Signal Construction Company (African American Division)
118th Signal Radio Company
12th Field Artillery Observer Battalion

14*th* Field Artillery H.Q. Battery
775*th* Tank Destroyer Battery
809*th* Tank Destroyer Battery
810*th* Tank Destroyer Battery
633*rd* Tank Destroyer Battery
829*th* Tank Destroyer Battery
68*th* Medical Regiment
92*nd* Ordnance Company
108*th* Ordnance Company
78*th* Quartermaster Battalion
28*th* Quarter master Regiment (African American Division)
98*th* Engineer Battalion (African American Division)
184*th* Field Artillery (African American Division)
24*th* IM Car Company (African American Division)
580*th* Ordinance Company (African American Division)
365*th* Engineering Battalion (African American Division)
65*th* Quartermaster Battalion (African American Division)
366*th* Engineering Company (African American Division)
216*th* General Hospital
12*th* Station Hospital Unit
65*th* Medical Regiment
68*th* Medical Group
106*th* Station Hospital Unit
23*rd* Hospital Train
24*th* Hospital Train
1*st* Hospital Train
7*th* Hospital Train
331*st* Medical Group
39*th* Evacuation Hospital
106*th* Evacuation Hospital
109*th* Evacuation Hospital
116*th* Evacuation Hospital
46*th* Medical Depot Company
48*th* Medical Depot Company
4 Medical Sanitary Companies (Unit numbers unknown)
23*rd* Headquarters Special Troops (Ghost Army)
6888*th* Central Postal Directory Battalion

Construction

The federal government sent residents pamphlets regarding the impending construction in the area. Notices for submission of construction bids appeared in newspapers throughout Tennessee and Georgia. By October 1940, the War Department announced contract awards totaling $8,637,600 to Hardaway Contracting Company of Columbus, Georgia, and Creighton Company of Nashville, Tennessee. The two companies formed a partnership for the duration of the construction project. According to the Bureau of Labor Statistics, the contract is equivalent to $155,747,651 in 2018. The architectural and engineering contracts were awarded to Chicago-based Greeley and Hansen. The federal government awarded several other contracts to various vendors over the next two years for additional buildings, a 100,000-gallon water tank and tower and an airport.[19] The War Department's Office of the Constructing Quartermaster coordinated everything related to construction at the jobsite. Newspapers across the Southeast reported Quartermaster General Major Carl H. Brietwieser was in charge of the construction project, which commenced with clearing land and the delivery of building materials as its first projects. Construction crews launched building projects soon thereafter.

The population of Tullahoma exploded as men and families descended on the small town, eager to find work. Workers found food and shelter wherever they could, as shortages in town and the surrounding areas quickly became the norm. Numerous Middle Tennesseans participated in the dawn and eventual demise of Camp Forrest. Some men not only worked at the facility but also inducted and trained at it. In October 1940, Lee Beavers[20] headed to the train station to return to Bowling Green College of Commerce in Kentucky after visiting his sister, Jewell McGowen, for a few days. His curiosity piqued that bright sunny morning as he saw the huge crowd forming in the post office parking lot. The taxi driver pulled over so Lee could investigate the commotion. After Beavers pushed his way to the front of the crowd, the stout man by the small table underneath the tent asked him if he was interested in a job. The bright-eyed nineteen-year-old exclaimed, "Sure!" The stout man gave him directions to the jobsite, where he needed to report later that day for his first assignment. In returning to the cab, he exclaimed to the driver that he just got a job and to drive him to the address on the card. It was not until the next day that Beavers learned the stout man was Hardaway Construction Company's personnel director, Whitelaw R. Leath. Beavers was surprised when he arrived at the construction site, finding only a small building amid the huge pastures and wooded areas along the access road. The Camp Peay military reservation was located on the far side of the initial Camp Forrest construction site. Beavers envisioned a large company such as Hardaway Construction already having numerous truckloads of materials, equipment and men bustling about the site. Major Brietwieser was at the site when Beavers reported for work. Beavers's job was simple but extremely important: answer the phone and either take a message or find the person the caller asked for. Within three weeks of the publication of the construction employment announcements, thousands of individuals looking for work descended on the southern hamlet of Tullahoma. Soon, Beavers knew everyone employed at the site by name.

During the first couple of months of construction, the small contingent of workers built roads throughout the cantonment and filled mud pits and swampy areas with gravel. At the recommendation of the typing teacher at Shelbyville High School, James Spence[21] obtained a job building roads throughout Camp Forrest. Under the employ of Allen Duke, he received fifty cents per load of crushed gravel delivered to the construction site. His quota was delivering twelve truckloads of gravel during each twelve-hour night shift. The quota was attainable, but there was little time for meals, most certainly not for accidents or vehicle breakdowns. The roads were composed

Tullahoma boasted numerous stores, restaurants, movie theaters, USO clubs, banks, transportation options, recreational activities, churches and loads of southern hospitality for its new citizens. *Author's collection.*

of three-foot-deep crushed gravel. Tons of gravel sank to the bottom of the mud pits quickly. Numerous additional loads of gravel helped to eventually solidify the areas. The mud presented continual problems, as numerous dump trucks filled with crushed gravel never seemed to fill the swampy pits. Luckily, there were no reports of man, beast or machine being engulfed in the mud and never being seen again.

The initial full payday for the first 2,500 construction workers employed was October 25, 1940. The total payroll was $175,000 (approximately $3,140,413 in 2018).[22] Major Brietwieser reported to the media in 1941 that at the height of construction there were 22,000 workers on the payroll. Workers consisted of skilled laborers and semiskilled and unskilled workers. As construction neared completion, the workforce was reduced to 2,287 laborers. The Corps of Engineers set the pay rates for construction workers on military installations, which were generally higher than wages paid elsewhere. Beavers recalled carpenters earning $1.25 per hour (approximately $22.00 in 2018), common labor compensation $0.30 per hour (approximately $5.29 in 2018) and bulldozer and heavy equipment operators $1.40 per hour (approximately $25.00 in 2018). Some laborers, such as electricians, were unionized and compensated at a different rate. Many of the new unskilled workers to the area pretended to be carpenters, given the high rate of pay. Many did not possess tools of the trade and hastily purchased supplies from Lawson Hardware in downtown Tullahoma. The lack of experience of many individuals explains the construction anomalies occasionally discovered throughout the base's operation.

African Americans came to Tullahoma seeking employment during the construction phase. They held numerous skilled positions, such as carpenters, plumbers, cooks and railroad workers. A CCC camp established at Camp Forrest housed two hundred African Americans responsible for maintenance and beautification projects around the cantonment.[23] The African American community experienced a rapid increase in the opening of stores, restaurants, barbershops and beauty salons. The need for housing was equally problematic for this community. Most residents rented out all available space within their homes. Others built homes to accommodate the increasing population. The African American USO was located on South Jackson and Cook Streets.[24]

Construction on Camp Forrest began in October 1940, and workers had a majority of the installation built within six months. Bob Couch recalled around-the-clock construction occurring in harsh winter conditions. Some individuals employed were skilled laborers and members of their profession's labor union. However, many individuals had never held a hammer or screwdriver. Construction halted for several weeks later that year due to union disputes for overtime compensation rates.

After Washington and union officials reached an agreement in regards to an overtime compensation structure within a month, construction resumed.[25] The agreement stated in part that construction workers no longer worked on Sundays and that authorities were responsible for ensuring different laborers received the correct type of overtime (i.e., time and a half versus double time). In an effort to keep his budget in the black, Brietwieser and his team closely monitored overtime usage. A typical weekly payroll was $490,000 ($8,821,330 in 2018) for 8,400 workers, but at the height of construction in December 1940, it was $748,000 ($12,824,791 in 2018) for 21,400 workers.[26] The union disputes, lumber shortages and inclement weather ultimately caused significant construction delays. Construction slowed in December 1940 due to lumber shortages. It was widely reported in the media that less than half of the anticipated lumber supplies were received daily once construction work expanded. Lumber became the preferred building material, as defense industries needed all available forms of metal-produced war goods. Delivery of lumber supplies eventually returned to normal, and construction continued unabated.[27] The construction ran two months behind schedule, which pushed the arrival of regiments from Colorado, Tennessee and Illinois to Camp Forrest until mid-March 1941 instead of January.

During the end of the construction phase, governmental contract awards went to local companies and individuals to provide the base with various food and material supplies. A local cooperative founded in 1936, Duck River Electric Membership Corporation won the contract to provide electricity throughout the base. Gray's Garage won the contract to provide gasoline, kerosene and oil for the base's twenty-three service stations. Local farmers and dairies provided fruits, vegetables, cheese and milk as part of the army's grocery supply.

Although the cantonment was only 95 percent completed, the troops began arriving by train and truck convoys. However, with the 33rd Division's arrival in March, the mud was so bad that the men had to construct wood catwalks before they could leave the gravel road to reach their barracks.[28] After his first week at Camp Forrest, the commander of the 191st Field Artillery, Harry Berry, sent a message to his successor at the Tennessee WPA, Simpson Tate Pease of Memphis, that read in part, "Suggest WPA project. Please send 30,000 workers to dig 30,000 soldiers out of the mud."[29]

Left: Raised wooden sidewalks or catwalks, a common site, allowed soldiers to avoid having to traverse the mud. *Author's collection.*

Below: Rains turned the Tennessee red clay into a sea of mud, but overshoes and catwalks helped to mitigate the problem. *Author's collection.*

Soldiers found that, sometimes, the electrical and plumbing at the base did not work properly, given the cantonment was built so quickly. Soldiers recalled the afternoon when an unfortunate GI learned that a plumber had improperly hooked up hot water to a toilet. The hospital treated the resulting steam burns promptly. In later years, Dudley Tipps[30] attempted to recycle bricks from the cantonment but found that workers used cement rather than mortar.

The War Department decided in January 1941 to change the base's name from Camp Peay to Camp Forrest, in honor of the famed Confederate general Nathan Bedford Forrest. Many individuals, including the 33rd Division commander, General Samuel Tilden Lawton of Illinois, protested the proposed change. News reports indicated that the adjutant general of Tennessee, Brigadier General Thomas A. Frazier, a native of Chattanooga, proposed the name when the War Department requested suggestions. Angry letters and protests inundated the War Department based on General Forrest's controversial exploits at Fort Pillow during the Civil War and the fact he was a slave trader. Others, including Tennessee Governor Cooper, said it was appropriate to name the facility after Forrest, as he was one of the greatest cavalrymen and was born in the neighboring town of Chapel Hill.[31] To quell the protest, the War Department indicated it would consider other possibilities, but the name soon thereafter became official.[32] In a radio broadcast, Mary Forrest Bradley, the only granddaughter of General Forrest, spoke of her recent trip to review the base and the troops stationed there.[33] She found the facility and the troops quite impressive.

TULLAHOMA RESPONDS TO CONSTRUCTION PHASE

Infrastructure of Tullahoma was not equipped to deal with the sudden influx of people during construction or the arrival of soldiers and their family members. Nevertheless, there was a war going on, so the population of forty-five hundred rose to the occasion, renting rooms, cooking for soldiers and visitors and assisting in military efforts when appropriate. The town soon became the fifth-largest population center in Tennessee. Mayor Don Campbell, city aldermen and other businesspersons worked to alleviate these infrastructure problems as quickly as possible. Mayor Campbell began taking steps to increase the police force and enlarge the city's water and lighting companies based on the anticipated growth.[34]

Some likened the construction work on the outskirts of town to a beautiful symphony. With so many workers busy on so many different projects, it is difficult to understand why chaos did not pervade throughout the encampment. Once a foundation cured, the crew moved to the next job, and the work in the area switched to the sounds of carpenter crews pounding nails. As sections of each building were completed, the crews moved into place to hoist the skeletal walls into position. Once the bare exterior walls were erected, the skilled labor of electricians and plumbers moved into place to ply their trades. Finishing carpenters completed interior work, and the building was ready for occupancy. At another end of the compound, several railroad crews were preparing to install spurs from the main track. From these railroad spurs, trains brought supplies to the quartermaster division. Each day, crews finished sections of the massive metropolis.

Up and Away Into the Wild Blue...Construction of Northern Field

Northern Field, operational by 1942, was located about five miles from Camp Forrest. It was the training ground for the Seventy-First Army Air Force, a detachment of the 737 Army base, the Blue Ribbon Airborne Division and the Seventeenth Airborne Division.[35] The base provided areas for pilots to practice flying B-24s and observation planes and for paratroopers to jump. The base underwent several name changes: Camp Forrest Airdrome, Tullahoma Army Air Base and, finally, William Northern Army Air Field. On November 11, 1942, amid a military ceremony, the army dedicated the Tullahoma Army Air Base in honor of Second Lieutenant William Lee Northern Jr., who was the first Tennessean causality of World War II. The native of Nashville perished on December 21, 1941, in a midair collision with another army plane while on patrol duty over the Pacific Ocean off the coast of California. Northern was a member of the Ninety-Fourth Fighter Squadron. Attendees at the dedication ceremony included dignitaries from throughout the state, as well as his parents, Mr. and Mrs. William Northern Sr., his fiancée and classmate Jeanne Fennville, Governor Cooper, Major General Joseph Patch (formally in command of the Eightieth Division), Brigadier General Arthur McDaniel of the Third Air Force and Colonel and Mrs. Scott, base commander of the new airfield and his wife. During the ceremony, the Vanderbilt Chapter of Sigma Chi

Fraternity, of which young Northern was a member, presented a white floral cross in his memory and scattered roses across the airfield. Members of the Eightieth Division fired a ten-gun salute.[36]

The $1.4 million airfield had three five-thousand-foot concrete runways, barracks, mess halls and administrative buildings. Northern Field had its own recreation hall, movie theater, mess hall, PX, machine shops, hospital, classrooms, service clubs and restaurant, commanding officer and civilian administrative offices and a base personnel administrative office. It had movies, concerts and USO shows similar to those at Camp Forrest. The official newspaper for the base was the *Northeraire*. In the July 1943 inaugural issue, the commanding officer, Colonel C.C. Scott, remarked on the hard work and successes achieved to meet the needs of modern aerial warfare. Denoting the complexity of the training process, soldiers were required to "master the intricate problems of gunnery, navigation, precision bombing and aerial observation…studying a multitude of technical, scientific and military data."[37]

Review of the soldiers of the 788th A.A.A. (A.W.) NN at William Northern Field in March 1944. *Author's collection.*

Observation planes flying overhead were a common site in the Middle Tennessee skies as pilots practiced the skills of identifying areas and objects on the ground. *Author's collection.*

At the end of 1942, the bombing and gunnery range for the facility was operational. This portion of the facility trained pilots in aerial bombardment and low-level attack. Crews spent several months creating targets, strafing objects, shooting and creating fire-control mechanisms.[38] Many residents remember large sacks of either flour or corn meal falling from Tullahoma skies as B-24 Liberators practiced hitting targets. The sacks simulated the weight of bombs the pilots would be carrying overseas. From these simulations, the aviators could better understand how to control a plane weighed down with bomb loads. During maneuvers, planes dropped "flour bombs" on troops to add to the reality of the moment. It was easy to detect the soldiers who were "victims" of aerial bombs, as each man was covered in flour. This tactic remained an effective teaching tool, as soldiers learned to spot and take cover from incoming ordnances quickly.[39] Several residents recalled looking for "unexploded" bags of flour and corn meal and carrying them home. The army's requisitions of these staples caused a tremendous shortage throughout the area. Work seemingly continued efficiently and effectively amid the continual housing shortages.

Housing Problems

Housing became an immediate problem once construction on Camp Forrest commenced. As workers rented available rooms in Tullahoma and neighboring towns, several tent cities and trailer camps sprang up. Entrepreneurial out-of-towners purchased or leased land near the cantonment to erect these tent cities to provide food and lodging for workers. Newcomers to the area would visit the local board of trade office to determine available housing opportunities. This office also worked to ensure price gouging in the area did not occur. Individuals who engaged in such activities could face fines and/or legal action. The location and amenities offered for a rented room varied greatly. In addition to a room, some property owners, such Mrs. Dunn in Granville, offered renters one to three meals a day. She purchased eggs, beans and meats wholesale so she could feed everyone. Although her husband was a carpenter at Camp Forrest, the $8 per week (approximately $141 in 2018) paid by each of the eight boarders living at their home was enough to pay all of the monthly household expenses. The family was able to save Mr. Dunn's wages for a rainy day. However, this situation did not represent the norm, as most proprietors provided only a room for an identical rate.[40]

Individuals unable to secure a room slept in cars, barns, smokehouses and citizens' yards. Some individuals quit and returned home after being unable to obtain any form of housing. Movie theaters ran twenty-four hours a day and allowed some individuals to sleep there when other accommodations were unavailable. Often, workers would sleep in empty

TENNESSEE
AIR CONDITIONED
CABINS
FOR RENT !

BY THE DAY OR BY THE HOUR
KNEE ACTION WITH FLOATING POWER
OVER SIZED HOLES - TWO CATALOGUES
A NICE QUIET PLACE TO SIT AND THINK
RATES REASONABLE

Renters soon learned there was no standard price for room and board. Some property owners also included three home-cooked meals per day. *Marjorie Collier collection.*

boxcars at train yards. Sleeping in boxcars was risky for heavy sleepers, as the makeshift boudoir was likely to hook up to a locomotive destined for a faraway city. Lee Beavers recalled several construction workers missing work for a few days because they awoke in Chattanooga. The men had to figure out a quick, inexpensive way to get back to Tullahoma! In another instance, he recalled that two men were taking a quick siesta in an attic crawlspace. When they awoke, the ceiling was finished and they were unable to leave. Passing workers heard their cries and were able to cut a hole in the ceiling, allowing them to exit the "tomb."

Federal authorities began studying the housing shortage problem to determine the best course of action to eliminate the problem. Everyone realized that the problem would only increase as troops and their families began to entrain to the area. Many military and city leaders met to discuss concerns and possible solutions to the housing crisis.[41] Almost a year and a half after the study and this meeting, the Federal Housing Authority, headquartered in Atlanta, awarded a contract to the Mobile Company to construct a seventy-five-unit apartment complex and one hundred war-efficiency houses for workers at Camp Forrest and Northern Field. The new communities, located three-quarters of a mile west of Tullahoma, were built at an estimated cost of $326,400 (about $4,727,885 in 2018).[42]

Within the first four months of 1941, twenty new businesses opened and there were now thirty-two new residences and two apartment buildings under construction.[43] Numerous restaurants and cafés opened to accommodate the flood of people to the area. Some proprietors of these establishments had prior food-service experience, but many did not. Military commanders and base physicians worked with city officials routinely to inspect each establishment and their food-safety and handling practices. The federal government was not inclined to have its service members or industry workers become ill due to inadequate and improper food-safety practices. Several establishments did not meet army standards and were declared "off bounds," which prohibited soldiers from frequenting them.[44]

The town's welcoming receptions grew as troops continued to arrive. Camp Forrest officially opened in March 1942, although construction on the reservation continued. The only furniture store in town, Rollins & Levan Furniture Company, had a difficult time maintaining stock with the second wave of newcomers to town. Homeowners were converting every possible space in their homes to rent, from dining rooms to sunrooms. Store manager Bill Hawkersmith reported to *Tennessean* journalist Randolph Tucker[45] that

The General Café was located across from the General Shoe Corporation factory. The Otwell family owned and operated the café. *Maxine Dean family collection.*

Hawkersmith family photo (*front to back, right to left*): newborn Betty Sue, Christine, Joanne, William and Louis. *Joanne H. Roberson family collection.*

One of three trolley cars purchased by the city after Nashville discontinued its trolley service and donated cars and tracks to the war effort. *Tullahoma Fine Arts Center.*

beds, dressers and bureaus were flying out the front door. The King Hotel purchased the bulk of his last shipment. Although the hotel had seventy-five rooms, fifty baths and a coffee shop, it had recently converted a portion of its dining room into temporary bedrooms. It was operating beyond capacity.[46] During one visit to the downtown furniture store, Hawkersmith's three-year-old daughter, Joanne, was amazed at the rows of hope chests stacked floor to ceiling. It was customary for young brides to place their wedding trousseau and other belongings in a hope chest. Hawkersmith's purchase was a prudent business decision, given the anticipated increase in nuptial ceremonies. New businesses sprang up in the most unlikely of places. Al Turesky and his wife came from Chattanooga to rent space in Taylor's Drug Store. They sold jewelry and various souvenirs to customers.[47] Three trolley cars purchased from Nashville contractors became lunchrooms and a mobile bar. The cars became available for purchase by the public and businesses when Nashville ceased operating its streetcar lines. Residents recalled that one trolley car was a mobile café serving sandwiches and hamburgers and a second one was a mobile "hooch wagon" that had a counter and spinning barstools.

Civilian Workers

During the construction phase, it came as a surprise to the mayor, many city officials and Hardaway-Creighton Company supervisors that there were so few instances of trouble, gambling and drunkenness from construction workers or townspeople. This was a remarkable feat, given the town's population almost tripled in a short time frame.[48] As construction neared completion, the number of workers fell to 2,287. The construction phase officially ended on April 1, 1941. As the encampment started becoming operational, the need to employ civilian personnel became paramount. The camp civilian personnel officer, Lieutenant Ben Levy, indicated that the greatest needs were for laundry workers, bakers and nurses.[49] More than 12,000 civilian employees worked at Camp Forrest throughout the war. Civilians filled these positions so that able-bodied men could join the fight overseas.

In the summers, high school student Eddie Sherber[50] worked in one of the various motor pools at Camp Forrest. His main responsibilities were to address major vehicle issues, such as radiator holes and burned-up motors. The motor pool also had numerous separate vehicle divisions: motorcycles, tires, salvage and small and large parts warehouses. Several POWs also worked in the motor pool throughout his time at Camp Forrest. One POW whom Sherber befriended was a college graduate who spoke fluent English. Before the war, the man had been a professional soccer player.

Seth Sharbur[51] held numerous positions at Camp Forrest and Northern Field throughout World War II. He initially worked as a mechanic's helper when the base officially opened but transferred to the rail yard and learned to operate a twenty-ton engine. The engine was responsible for bringing boxcars to and from the base via a spur off the main railroad line. Each day, approximately ten to twenty boxcars of goods and supplies arrived and were dispersed to the various warehouses on base. Approximately forty to fifty of the cavalry battalion's horses arrived from Ohio via railway. The cavalry was still active until mid-1942, when it transitioned to a mechanized division. Horses and mules were no longer necessary when the base fully mechanized. Railcars transported many of the animals home, but some of them met premature deaths. Employees, such as William Brasier, recall them being led to a trench and shot. The exact details and reasons for this act are unknown, but it was extremely disturbing and upsetting. Seth Sharbur ended his tenure at Camp Forrest in the motor pool as an inspector. After road construction, James Spence also worked in the motor pool before joining the U.S. Army Air Corps. In that role, he maintained a vehicle parts warehouse and filled requisition orders. After he enlisted, he served with the Fifth Division in the southwest Pacific. Although he held numerous positions during his military career, he most fondly recalls being the secretary to a Colonel Fitzgerald.[52]

The need for greater telephone capacity in town and on the base rose dramatically as the population soared. Myrtle Pearsol[53] became a switchboard operator at Camp Forrest and then Northern Field. Before the construction phase, there were only 500 residential and business telephones in the greater Tullahoma area. The immediate installation of an additional 150 lines was necessary to ensure adequate communication between construction site offices. These additions taxed the town's current system, necessitating upgrades. Over a six-month period, the single operator office grew exponentially to include sixteen operators to maintain the increased call volume. On the base, ten trained operators ran that exchange, which had 800 lines available. Over twenty-five miles of telephone lines hung throughout the camp. Two telegraph companies set up operations for the camp.[54] According to the Camp Forrest telephone directory, each line was for specific administrative purposes. Class A lines were for official business only and had access to city trunk lines for that

NAME:	No.	NAME	No.
QUARTERMASTER (CONT.)		**SPECIAL SERVICES (CONT.)**	
Subsistence Section:		Theater Officer	179
Cold Storage Officer	47	Theater No. 1	299
Commissary Sales Store	534	Theater No. 2	367
Commissary Office	320	Theater No. 3	368
Commissary Officer	321	Theater No. 4	482
Perishables Warehouse	584		
Refrigeration Engineer	570	**STATION HOSPITAL**	
Sales Commissary (Clerk)	551		
Sales Commissary Office	795	Adjutant	26
Unit Supply	280	Army Personnel	533
Warehouse, Classification	351	Barracks D-16	415
Warehouse, Reclamation	554	Chaplain	450
Warehouse, Commissary	357	Chief of Medical Service	71
Warehouse, #154	455	Chief Nurse	56
Warehouse, Officer	110	Chief of Surgical Service	553
Warehouse, Receiving	113	Commanding Officer	228 & 459
Warehouse, Vegetables	584	Convalescent Camp	156
		Dental Clinic #1	28
RED CROSS		Dental Clinic #2	304
		Detachment Med. Dept.	485 & 69
Administration	134	Detachment Mess	336
Hospital	99	Detachment Supply Officer	350
		Deiticians Office	94
SCHOOL FOR BAKERS & COOKS		E.E.N.T. Clinic	81
		Examining Office	56
Administration Office	334	G. U. Clinic	87
Senior Instructor Office	285	Heating Plant	70
		Information	54 & 402
SIGNAL OFFICE		Laboratory	303
		Medical Supply Officer	132
Chief Operator	0	Medical Supply Whse	432
Communications Message Center	431	Mess Officer	403
Film Librarian	441	Mess Storeroom	332
Requisition Clerk	102	Morgue	327
Signal Officer	22 & 359	Nurses' Mess	78
Signal Property	317	Nurses' Quarters	
Signal Repair Shop	205	#1	58
Signal Warehouse	122	#3	59
Telegraph Office	100	#4	75
Telephone Accounts	266	#5	491
~~WVBE~~	~~430~~	#6	44
		#7	369
SPECIAL SERVICES		Officers' Quarters	60 & 265
		Operating Room	68
Guest House	278	Orthpedic Clinic	67
Senior Hostess	279	Patients Mess #1	94
Guest House #2 (Colored)	347	Patients Mess #2	62
Officers Club	364	Pharmacy	76
Reception Office, Colored		Post Exchange	383
Recreational Area	497	Post Office	446
Service Club	279	Receiving Office	387 & 532
Special Services Officer	170	Red Cross	99
Sports Arena	590		
Theater Office	178		

This page of the Camp Forrest telephone directory contains extensions for the Red Cross, various quartermaster areas, the Station Hospital, the Signal Office and Special Services divisions. *Author's collection.*

purpose. Class B lines were for personal use and had access to city trunk lines for that purpose. Class C was restricted to calls within the camp. Class D lines were for special services, such as fire alarms, guard alarms and watchman services. The caller and the operator had to know these classifications. Units were responsible for prompt payment for telephone usage, as Uncle Sam did not foot the bill for calls.

Pearsol was a perfect switchboard operator candidate, given her experience using such equipment while living in nearby McMinnville. Operators could not have any form of food or drink near the switchboard, as spills could result in expensive repairs. She would watch the young switchboard operators eat hurriedly and dash back to their posts when they frequented her husband's café. They offered to teach her the telephone trade so they could enjoy longer breaks. The Pearsol family eventually moved to Tullahoma, where Myrtle obtained a switchboard operator position and the General Shoe Corporation hired her husband. They also rented rooms to seven boarders. In her proprietor experience, the boarders often had free rein of the home, as she and her husband worked second and third shifts, and their daughter attended South Jackson School during the day. The rent included only a room, but Myrtle remembered that boarders would often help themselves to items in the refrigerator. She was the first civilian hired at Northern Field and remained there for three years. She was one of the last civilian personnel employed before the airport closed in 1945. She was awarded a service medal for her time at the complex. Initially, the switchboard at Northern Field was small, but it expanded to a very large one requiring three to four operators working two shifts.

Manda Limbaugh's[55] first job at Camp Forrest was working at the hospital, bringing juice to patients. She eventually transferred to the officers' mess and remained there for two years. There were generally five to six workers on each of the two daily shifts. During that time, on her off days, she enjoyed attending the movie theater on base and listening to POW bands play on Sunday afternoons. Manda spoke of a sixteen-year-old German POW whom she and other female employees protected a little bit more since he was so young. One POW made her a silver necklace in exchange for a pack of cigarettes.

Frank Grant[56] joined the army as soon as he graduated high school in Galveston, Texas, in 1940. He worked as an MP at Gate 1 at Camp Forrest. During his first month in Tullahoma, he recalled the waist-deep snow everywhere. After several months, he transferred to the motor pool. He enjoyed the small-town atmosphere and met his future wife, Marian Martin

GENERAL SHOE CORP.
Tullahoma, Tenn.

300th

General Hospital

Camp Forrest, Tenn.

Thanksgiving = 1942

Above: The General Shoe Corporation won a $1,300,000 ($18,722,823 in 2018) contract to produce and repair military shoes brought from Camp Forrest. *Author's collection.*

Left: The 1942 menu for the 300th General Hospital Thanksgiving. The inside contains the name of each soldier in the regiment and the foods served for that event. *Author's collection.*

of Tullahoma, during his time at the base. They dated for the next year and married in December 1945. Although most of the soldiers had left the base by 1944, he also worked part time at the noncommissioned officers' club. He worked the snack bar, and POWs worked in the kitchen. Even after his discharge in late August 1945, he went on war bond tours in local high schools, telling students about the war and encouraging them to support it through the purchase of bonds.

During her days off from Camp Forrest, Eva Jean Hindman[57] was a frequent customer of the downtown café Kandy Kitchen. Since it was close to the bus station, she met many military spouses and girlfriends who arrived in Tullahoma from other states. The café was typically one of the first stops for weary out-of-state visitors. Many of these women did not have friends or relatives in town, they had no place to stay and they were unsure how to reach their loved ones at Camp Forrest. Most of the establishments offering lodging, such as the King Hotel, traditional boardinghouses and the base guest housing and hotel were typically booked. She drove the visitors around town until they were able to locate a homeowner with a room to rent. Meeting Eva Jean was many of these individuals' first encounters with southern hospitality!

Dewy Smith[58] was a base military police officer from January 1943 to December 1945. Each division had MPs, as did the base itself. The base MPs were responsible for directing traffic and patrolling the base proper and surrounding roads. The MPs would periodically review a soldier's pass to ensure it was authentic and had not expired. The penalty for being off base without permission could range from kitchen police (KP) duty to a demotion. The four base MPs worked twelve-hour shifts, seven days a week. Smith was also in charge of finding and picking up soldiers in the area who had been classified as AWOL (absent without official leave). Military headquarters in Atlanta sent notices to Camp Forrest of AWOL soldiers. Many men deemed AWOL were soldiers who had permission to leave but had simply not returned before their pass expired. During his time as a base MP, Smith picked up approximately three hundred AWOL soldiers. The soldiers were booked and held at the nearest jail and were eventually picked up by another division for prosecution. Camp Forrest had twelve guardhouses and two large stockades. The AWOL soldier who Smith did not immediately return was a young man whose baby daughter was extremely sick at the local hospital. After verifying the baby's illness with the hospital, Smith waited two weeks before returning to the soldier's home. The baby had recovered, and the soldier returned to his division. His most memorable

Tullahoma's city hall, fire department and jail. An additional temporary jail built under the city's viaduct also housed criminals. *Author's collection.*

experience was being a part of the escort party during one of President Roosevelt's visits to Camp Forrest.

Richard Radock recalled the flurry of activity about the encampment before the presidential review of the division commenced. Not only were the troops preparing, but the "Secret Service agents checked all of the weapons and artillery pieces, mortars, etc. to make sure they were not loaded."[59]

Civilian firefighters protected the base during the construction phase. Those men were relieved of their duty by the 108th Ordnance Company when construction was finished. The fire marshal, Lieutenant Colonel Merlin Bruce, had oversight of the five stations located throughout the cantonment. Although several fires occurred over the years on the base, there are no reports of major damages or loss of life. In one barracks fire, numerous soldiers lost military and personal possessions. The military reissued all government items at no charge, and the Red Cross replaced most of the destroyed personal items. The quick response of the fire trucks prevented further destruction to surrounding buildings. The cause of the fire was undetermined.

Clennie Huddleston[60] moved to the area from Jasper, Alabama, to obtain a job with a lumber company. He was soon unemployed, but he was able to secure a job as a manager of one of the post exchanges at Camp Forrest. On a typical day, Huddleston would ensure the PX was clean and well stocked with inventory before soldiers began to arrive. Two janitors from the 107th

Firefighters quickly extinguished the barracks fire on April 7, 1941. Reports indicate there was minimal damage to the building's contents and structure. *NARA-CP.*

Calvary PX helped ensure everything was in order each morning. He earned $125.00 per month as a PX manager. Each PX utilized a checks-and-balances system to protect against theft or fraud. Utilizing this system, an army officer worked with PX managers to ensure there was either a receipt indicating a sale or that the inventory was on the shelf. The base mailed the completed reports to a main PX commission. Huddleston did not realize there was a $400.00 (equal to approximately $6,000.00 in 2018) allowance for overages or shortages. This buffer was to cover acts beyond the manager's control: spoilage, shoplifting, breakage. Each PX at Camp Forrest was similar to an old-fashioned general store selling a variety of goods via its three sections: merchandise, fountain and beer. The merchandise section sold items such as watches, scarfs, stationery supplies, toiletries or souvenirs to send home. The fountain section sold cokes, candies, cookies and ice cream; the beer section sold ice-cold draft beer. The inventory came from local suppliers, and reports helped discern the merchandise obtained from each supplier. This inventory control method helped authorities quickly discern the supplier of candy that contained ground glass. Twenty soldiers were in serious to fatal condition and required hospitalization at Camp Forrest after ingesting tainted candy.[61] During his time at the PX, Huddleston's receipts were short a maximum of $4.26. He resigned his position, as he received his draft notice for induction into the U.S. Army Air Corps. The Camp Forrest hospital conducted his induction physical examination. He returned to the base as a warehouse employee after his discharge from the service.

Edna Conway[62] was in high school, but she and her sister worked in a PX after school and on weekends. Once a week, she worked the Northern Field PX. The only job in the PX she was not permitted to perform was pouring beer, which required a bartender of legal age. There were no significant disturbances on base during her employment. One afternoon, several male soldiers learned that recruits from the Women's Army Auxiliary Corps (WAAC) would soon arrive. She could tell by their tone and facial expressions they were displeased the army now allowed women soldiers. The WAAC recruits were trained in noncombat roles by 1942. Many Americans opposed women enlisting in the army; prevailing social norms deemed it "unladylike" behavior. The female soldiers received the same basic and advanced training as their male counterparts. Amid lower pay, less benefits and continual slanderous allegations, the women answered the call to serve their nation. Edna's cousin worked at one of the base guesthouses next to the service center. When rooms were available, she and several other girls would stay on base. Some of her most memorable times was attending dances and playing on the Camp Forrest softball team. She played first base and generally practiced on the base's baseball field. The team won most of its games and traveled overnight to Georgia for a playoff tournament game. Camp Forrest had men's and women's sponsored sports teams comprising military and civilian players. These various sports teams played against other military base teams as well as local college and business teams.

Joe Getsay[63] arrived at Camp Forrest in late 1943 and held several positions during his tenure at post headquarters. There were still numerous troops training on base when he arrived. He worked with POWs to repair targets at the Cumberland Springs firing range. He found the POWs he worked with were respectful and hardworking. He also worked as an MP, held a position in the laundry and coached the Camp Forrest men's basketball team. As an MP, he patrolled the perimeter of the base and provided traffic control in the mornings and afternoons. The traffic jams at the Camp Forrest gates decreased once the second exit near Estill Springs opened. His team played games against the Nashville Business College, Manchester Independent

Soldiers enjoying some recreational time playing basketball. Commanders encouraged soldiers to play sports, as it fostered teamwork and built stamina. *Author's collection.*

team and various other teams throughout the state. His future wife played on the women's basketball team. They talked on the bus rides to games and started dating soon thereafter. She lived in Beach Grove, about twenty-five miles away. So, he would hitchhike to see her, as he did not have a car.

James Pickett[64] worked at Camp Forrest before and after his time in the service. He and four other people worked in the salvage warehouse. The warehouse received army-issue fatigues and uniforms deemed unrepairable. The employees cut worn clothes into rags using an axe. He recalled that many of the clothes appeared in good shape and would be good to donate to people in the community. There were so many clothes cut each day, the rag piles were often as high as ten feet every couple of hours. POWs assigned to the division worked for him cutting clothes. He befriended one English-speaking POW. The prisoner enjoyed showing Pickett photos of his family members back home in Germany. The federal government required that brass belt buckles of soldiers' uniforms be removed and mailed to a headquarters division for reuse. The leather was eventually shredded. Knives and sharp blades given to POWs each day were collected before they left the facility.

In February 1941, Paul Boswell[65] transferred from a Tennessee National Guard unit in nearby Winchester to Camp Forrest. While stationed there, he encountered shortages of equipment, such as rifles. Rather than lose valuable training time, the men in his division practiced with wood rifles. Accounts of the shortages and out-of-date weapons appeared in the *Chicago Tribune* in late March 1941. The reports indicated the majority of the available supplies of infantry and artillery weapons were inadequate and outmoded in comparison to those currently used on the front.[66] After equipment arrived a few weeks later, the men were able to practice with new, modern weapons. He and his battery shipped out to the West Coast a week after December 7.

Husband and wife Russell and Ruby Kelly[67] worked at Camp Forrest from the construction phase until its decommissioning. Russell's father and two uncles worked there as well, as carpenters. They helped build barracks and finish the inside of one of the theaters. Russell joined Ruby working in the laundry after construction was completed. Both remembered many German POWs working in the facility who spoke fluent English. Both remembered that one of the POWs commented that he never wanted to fight in the war; the Nazi regime had forced him to join the German military. Most of the Camp Forrest POWs shared this sentiment.

Melvin and Eva Jean Hindman[68] lived on an Alabama farm when construction began. Melvin secured work on base clearing land for the construction projects. When construction was completed, he built furniture for the base. Like many families in the area, the Hindmans had several immediate and extended family members employed at the cantonment. Eva Jean's sister worked in the laundry, and her brother, Billy, worked at the bowling alley. The bowling alley on base had six lanes and was open daily from 2:00 p.m. to 10:00 p.m. There were several bowling teams, and tournaments were held over the years. She recalled that alleys did not have electric pinsetters; POWs reset pins by hand after each frame. A small PX provided beverages, and there were several bleachers for spectators.

One of Euther Chesser's first jobs was selling newspapers to soldiers on base. He eventually obtained a position with Columbia Dairy as a driver. One of his main responsibilities was delivering milk to the encampment as well as to troops in the field on maneuvers. During one delivery, he was stuck

Rifle range practice. The ability to shoot a multitude of weapons was key to ensuring the troops returned from the front with zero to minimal bullet wounds. *Author's collection*.

in a long line of cars waiting for a military convoy to pass. He proceeded to the front of the line of waiting cars and persuaded the soldier to let him pass. He told the recruit it was imperative the soldiers received their milk as soon as possible! He was drafted into the navy in 1944. He saw combat in Europe and Asia before the war ended.[69]

Orala Lelchty[70] obtained a job as a maintenance electrician during the construction phase in mid-1941. He was responsible for trouble-shooting any electrical and lighting problems. He also worked with and around German POWs without incident, although an MP escort was required if he was near former Waffen-SS troop members. Lelchty spoke of how the devastation of war caused a divide between the members of a Shelbyville family of German descent. As the war overseas escalated, the wife of a Musgrave Pencil Company manager wanted to return to Germany. She felt it was the only viable option for their teenage son and daughter. The husband felt it would be best to stay in the United States. Unable to come to an agreement, the wife and the son returned to Germany; the husband and the daughter stayed in Shelbyville. Unfortunately, the German military conscripted the son into service on their return to the fatherland. U.S. forces captured him, and he became a Camp Forrest POW. In the meantime, the daughter obtained a job at Camp Forrest. The son eventually reunited with his sister and father, albeit he was not the same boy who had left years earlier. This type of situation may have occurred often. Watson Hensley recalled the story of a young German man who grew up in the United States but was conscripted into the German military during a family visit to Germany. After his capture by American forces, he became a POW detained at Camp Forrest. At the war's end, he was able to call his mother, who had been living stateside throughout the war. She supposedly passed out on learning her son had been a POW in the United States for most of the war.[71]

In addition to the civilians working at Camp Forrest, there were scores of volunteers who joined in the camaraderie and patriotism. Many in the community helped perform tasks, such as mending clothes, providing stationery, preparing home-cooked meals, arranging or chaperoning dances or just having a conversation with a soldier. Dot Watson recalled attending United Service Organizations (USO) dances chaperoned by her mother, Anabel Couch. Like many of the women in the community, her mother engaged in numerous volunteer activities. Most women viewed these acts as their patriotic duty.

The construction on the service clubs and library was completed in early 1941, and the morale officer of Camp Forrest began appointing hostesses, junior hostesses and a librarian to operate these divisions. Martha Lagrone, Thirty-Third Division Service Club, was the base librarian.[72] The service club hostess positions were paid jobs, unlike those at USOs, which were staffed by volunteers. These positions arranged continual wholesome activities on base for soldiers. These activities included dances, musical entertainment, sporting events, dinners and USO shows. Gladys Addington received notice from morale officer Major Willard Hayes that she was to report for duty as junior hostess for the Service Club on March 31, 1941. She left her high school teaching position and lived on base at the Hostess House. She obtained permission to outfit her room with her own furnishings. The other junior hostess was Cumi Campbell. The junior hostesses reported to Ann McClain, who served as senior hostess for the facility. The armed forces deemed these positions necessary, as ensuring wholesome activities were continually available on base for an average four thousand soldiers per day was a significant undertaking.

Soldiers received weekend leave from 4:00 p.m. Friday until 12:00 a.m. Sunday. Railroads provided multiple trains destined for Chattanooga and Nashville. The Cherokee and Consolidate bus lines had a station in Tullahoma, and there were 886 licensed taxis. Before the war, there were fewer than 6 cabs in Tullahoma, but everyone was eager to capitalize on the need to drive soldiers to and from town. Only those taxis that displayed a special Camp Forrest sticker and had the appropriate car insurance could gain entrance into the cantonment grounds. Given the size of the cantonment, taxi stations were set up throughout the facility. Soldiers could hire a taxi to transport them across the campus rather than walking long distances. Taxis also transported soldiers and civilians to and from town. General Lawton issued orders that forbade soldiers from engaging in ungentlemanly behavior as well as hitchhiking. Additionally, Lawton forbade soldiers from having cars on base, wearing civilian clothes and living off base except on weekends. He held to the belief that everyone was at Camp Forrest for training and not to have a good time.[73] Visitors were discouraged from making surprise visits, as soldiers needed ample time to request day passes. Learning that one was unable to visit a soldier after a thirteen-hour car ride was more than disappointing.

Business card for taxi cab driver Horace Gray. Taxis could operate inside the base and drive passengers to and from town. *Alan Gray collection.*

The Officers Club[74] was a grand facility that could hold up to four hundred occupants. There were tennis and badminton courts and barbecue pits outside of it. Inside the facility, soldiers could relax and play games, such as chess, Ping-Pong or checkers, or read current newspapers and magazines. The *Daily News-Journal*[75] reported that the Officers Club was formally opened by a fundraiser bridge tea hosted by several of the Camp Forrest commanding officers' wives: Mrs. Millard Waltz (wife of base commanding officer), Mrs. Samuel T. Lawton (wife of commander of Illinois Thirty-Third Division) and Mrs. H.B. McMurdo (wife of commander of base hospital). Over three hundred women from the surrounding area attended the event and raised more than $500 (approximately $8,027 in 2018) for the relief of families of killed or disabled soldiers.

TRANSPORTATION

Rail was the fastest and least-expensive way to travel in the 1940s. However, military needs took priority during the war, leaving citizens to stay home, wait until seats became available or find another mode of transportation. The Camp Forrest Quartermaster's Rail Transportation section was responsible for coordinating all troop and supply movements. The division required careful coordination and monitoring of expenses to ensure governmental coffers remained in the black. Many residents remember jaunts to the train station to greet arriving troops. Welcome banners hung in various areas throughout the train and bus stations and in the main streets in town, and bands played during the day as each troop train arrived.

Soldiers who traveled for personal reasons, whether on day trips or furloughs, were responsible for making their own arrangements and payments. However, the camp did request special pricing for soldiers interested in day trips to cities within the state. The typical materials the base received by rail included food, coal, gasoline, motor vehicles, ordnance supplies, clothing and building materials.[76] By the end of November 1942, requests submitted to the railroad commission called for an increase to the railroad rates for a basic ticket, to 2.2 cents for one-way tickets, and to 1.98 cents for a round-trip ticket. A member of the Thirty-Third Illinois Division would have likely taken the Nashville, Chattanooga & St. Louis train home to Chicago. The $10.20 round-trip rail ticket (approximately $164 in 2018) for the 515-mile journey from Camp Forrest would not have included any

Military band rehearsing. Many of the regimental bands played during parades, dances, war bond rallies and other special events on and off base. *NARA-CP*.

meals or sleeper car accommodations. During peak furlough times, the bus and rail tickets sold out quickly. However, this type of problem did not stop several enterprising young soldiers from Colorado from getting home. The eight men decided to hire a taxi for the 2,400-mile round trip to Denver, which was only slightly more expensive than the combined train fare for eight seats.[77] Round-trip Greyhound Bus fare from Dayton, Ohio, to Camp Forrest was comparable to rail ticket prices; it was $10.20 (approximately $164.00 in 2018).

Given the size of Camp Forrest, it was generally unrealistic to walk throughout the compound. A bus or taxi was available for personal use; a motor pool vehicle could be used for military business. Throughout its operation, the base motor pool required a tremendous number of workers with varied mechanical skills. A master sergeant from Camp Forrest recommended local mechanic Otis Price[78] for a position after he repaired the officer's car. In the truck maintenance division, Price was responsible for rebuilding engines and radiators and supervising a crew of eight hundred

German POWs. His boss was civilian George Nichols. German POWs who were clock makers prior to the war assisted in rebuilding and testing speedometers. Lloyd McMahan Sr.,[79] a mechanic, was able to fix any type of vehicle. As a chief inspector for the base, he traveled regularly from Knoxville to Chattanooga to Nashville to assess repairs for government vehicles. He added that his responsibility was to assess problems other mechanics were unable to diagnose on governmental vehicles. After the problem was diagnosed, he would explain how best to repair the vehicle. He proudly remarked that his employment at Camp Forrest lasted three years, six months and twenty-eight days.

William Brasier was a mechanic supervisor in the motor pool. In his division, he had two to three mechanics and ten POWs working for him. POWs were always interested in trading items they had either acquired or made themselves for packs or single cigarettes. Brasier would sometimes bring his younger brother to work on Saturdays so he could trade with POWs. William gave his brother several cigarettes which allowed him to barter with the POWS. A few of the brother's prized items bartered for were a pair of boxing gloves and a basketball. The talents of POWs often extended beyond the arts; one made Brasier a pair of false teeth. In spring 1947, William Brasier received a letter from former German POW Alfred Arbatzat. Arbatzat had been part of the grounds crew and reminded Brasier in the letter that he rode the lawnmowers. He was able to locate his family when he returned to Germany, and they were all doing well. However, the country itself was devastated because of the war. He was able to obtain a job with a local farmer. He asked for nothing more from Brasier than a return letter.[80]

LAUNDRY

The *Jackson Sun* indicated that the laundry facility on base would be cleaning and pressing an estimated forty-five thousand pounds of laundry per week. The camp laundry officer, Lieutenant O.K. Lay, pointed out that the 210-foot-by-270-foot building could accommodate two hundred workers. The well-appointed facility had the newest cleaning equipment available. The laundry brought to the facility was marked with each man's serial number to ensure items were returned to the appropriate person. The article noted the boiler in the adjacent building required thirty thousand pounds of coal per month and approximately five hundred pounds of salt daily to soften the water.[81]

Eva Jean Hindman[82] was a twenty-two-year-old homemaker when she decided to leave her native state of Alabama to join her husband, Melvin, in Tullahoma. She secured a job in the laundry and remembered the expansiveness of the entire facility. Although it was a large-scale operation, two shifts were necessary to keep up with demand. She was responsible for washing soldiers' clothes, bed sheets and towels, but, primarily, she marked each laundry item in the bags that soldiers dropped off. Modern dry cleaners use a similar process to mark clothing. Marking clothes was a job most employees did not want to perform for fear of becoming sick from being in contact with germs and bacteria on dirty clothes. Frequently, a soldier's clothes contained dirt, mud and/or blood from countless hours of training. The job, however, had rewards, as loose change and dollar bills left in pockets were fair game. The laundry returned personal items, such as jewelry and watches, to soldiers. Eva Jean worked in the laundry for two years. She earned $29 per week (approximately $466 in 2018) but could make that much or more collecting loose change. In one instance, a soldier left $200 in his pocket. Although it would have been a great windfall, she made sure the money made it back to the owner, since it was such a large amount.

Lillian Milbourn and her sister-in-law Margaret Anderson[83] both worked in the laundry on the third shift, which was from 12:00 a.m. to 8:00 a.m. Sometimes, it was difficult for them to sleep soundly during the day, so they would nap during their breaks. One evening, the quartermaster over the laundry stopped by and found a worker asleep. Rather than reveal she was napping during her break, the other workers explained that she was sick and needed to rest for a few minutes. The prior summer, Margaret toured the base on a school bus. The passengers could disembark the bus to see the cavalry horses at the stables. Initially, the base housed more than six hundred horses and mules. Margaret started working at Camp Forrest in 1943, posting tickets to customers and marking clothes for stains. Lillian started several months later, marking clothes as well; she eventually transferred to the washing area. Each worker was required to drink Epsom salts, which was supposed to draw toxins from the body acquired from handling dirty clothes. Lillian's husband was at Camp Forrest for basic training for six months and embarked for the front on January 15, 1942. They also checked pockets and kept the loose change left behind, which helped to supplement income. They lived fifteen miles away in Manchester

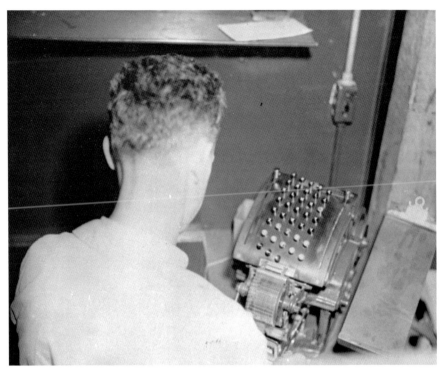

Marking machines placed the soldier's serial number on each item to ensure everything was returned to the appropriate person given the laundry's daily volume of business. *NARA-CP.*

and had to commute each day to work. Given rationing and shortages, items such as gasoline and tires required motorists like Lillian to always have numerous people carpooling with them. Prior to Camp Forrest, people in Manchester had limited employment options. Both women worked with numerous POWs while at the laundry and found them to be continually polite and respectful. They ruminated on the murder of Norma Faye Scogin and remembered how scared they were for several months thereafter, with thoughts they might meet the same fate. (This incident will be described in detail later in the chapter.)

As it was one of the largest employers at the base, many more people interviewed recalled their time as an employee in the laundry. Many said it was a wonderful place to work in the winter because of the heat produced by the massive washers, dryers and irons. While there was ventilation and fans in the facility, it could become very hot in the area during the summer months.

Station Hospital

Military hospitals had several classifications, based, in part, on the size of the base. Camp Forrest's medical facility classification was a Station Hospital, which rendered medical and surgical treatments for up to two thousand patients. The hospital area consisted of an administrative building, six nurses' quarters, two officers' quarters, an officers' mess, nine barracks, two clinics, one physiotherapy building, thirty-two wards, fire storehouses, one morgue, a central heating plant and the two-thousand-bed hospital. A full staff at the Station Hospital consisted of 60 physicians and 120 nurses, as well as hundreds of others in various support and administrative roles. The hospital was also one of the largest employers on base. However, when the medical staff reported for overseas duty, the facility became short staffed. The hospital admitted patients for a variety of physical or psychological reasons. Some of the minor injuries included sprains, respiratory infections and cuts. Serious medical cases included broken bones, gunshot wounds and surgeries. A majority of the records pertaining to Camp Forrest were destroyed when the St. Louis, Missouri National Archives Building burned in July 1973. The surviving records indicate the POW hospital provided 5,600 major operations, 21,000 X-rays and 120,000 physical therapy treatments by the end of 1945.[84]

The need for nurses increased exponentially as the war progressed. To help alleviate the shortage, the government turned to the Red Cross for help. Interested nurses could attain a military commission in the Army Nurse Corps. Red Cross nurse Mary Alice McKisset joined the service in late 1942. She remained stateside to assist the Vanderbilt Unit at the Station Hospital. She lived on base for the duration of the war and earned $200 per month, plus room and board. Her primary daily duties were overseeing patient care on specific wards. For a short period, she worked with patients in the psychiatric ward.

Lieutenant Carmella Paterniti Smith treated soldiers' physical and psychological wounds. Her care and devotion helped heal her patients' wounds more quickly. *Judy Jenkins collection.*

Most days were uneventful while she was on duty in this ward. However, one patient attempted to escape the base by stealing the keys to her Red Cross car. Luckily, MPs detained him at the main gates. McKisset routinely wrote letters home to family members for despondent patients and those unable to write. She also visited with her infirm patients' families staying at the Red Cross Guest House. As the base transitioned to a POW facility, she worked with several young Germans from the Black Forest. She also helped distribute Red Cross care packages to POWs throughout the base.[85]

Having recently completed her BS in chemistry at Tennessee Polytechnic Institute (Tennessee Tech) in Cookeville, Eileen Reeser Harkins[86] was asked by the chemistry department chair, Dr. Ferris Foster, if she was interested in working in the Camp Forrest laboratories. Being an army reservist, Dr. Foster was called to active duty and needed potential hospital technicians. Harkins accepted the offer and remained in the laboratory position for five years. There were approximately eighty people in the lab. A typical day consisted of drawing patients' blood and running tests. Some of the more typical tests she performed included measuring diabetic patients' blood sugar levels, performing blood counts and conducting pregnancy tests. Unlike today, these tests required considerable time to administer and evaluate.

Pregnancy tests in the 1940s required the injection of the patient's urine into a rabbit, a mouse or a frog. If the pregnancy hormone hCG was present in the woman's urine, the sexually immature animal's ovaries would be stimulated. Generally, interpretation of the results occurred after someone euthanized the animal. The test was approximately 98 percent accurate, but false positives were possible. From these tests, the phrase "rabbit died" came to be used to signify that a woman was pregnant. The medical community devised another method for measuring hCG hormones by the 1950s that did not require animal dissection.

One of the unfortunate aspects of Harkins's job was taking deceased patients to the morgue, which was located near the woods at the far end of the medical complex. Although the death rate was not extremely high, she did indicate that one soldier died of malaria. While uncommon in the United States today, it was possible for the World War II soldier on maneuvers throughout the southeastern region to contract malaria. It was not until the mid-1940s that aggressive efforts to eradicate the disease, which was contracted from mosquito bites, began in the United States. Soldiers received quinine, but commanding officers cautioned soldiers to use mosquito nets on beds, as the insect was more prone to bite at night.[87] In addition to the enemy, mosquitoes, ticks, chiggers and rodents, soldiers had

Soldier holding two large snakes while on maneuvers in Tennessee. Soldiers had to be mindful of snakes, insects and the enemy. *Author's collection*.

to watch their step to ensure there were no snakes underfoot. Tennessee has thirty-four species of snakes, of which four are venomous.

Reeser Harkins[88] earned $135 per month and lived in the hospital's nursing quarters until she married Leroy Harkins. Her husband served in the Medical Service Corps and shipped out to France to set up field hospital laboratories a year after their marriage. As the camp transitioned to a POW facility, Eileen had the opportunity to work with numerous German captives. Each prisoner she encountered was curious and wanted to learn as much as possible about U.S. medical services. Due to the presence of the prisoners, base policy required an armed guard to escort Harkins to and from her laboratory each day. Her father worked in the heavy equipment division at Camp Forrest. As was customary in most households around the base, her family routinely brought soldiers to their home for meals and socializing.

The Couch family rented rooms to numerous out-of-town visitors and Camp Forrest employees. Dot Couch Watson[89] fondly remembers a young nurse stationed at Camp Forrest who rented a room at the family home for several months. The nurse made the toddler Dot a nurse's outfit and always had time to play. Dot acknowledges the impact this woman had on her life and credits her decision to pursue her three-decade career in the healthcare field to her.

In 1939, Carmella Paterniti Smith[90] became a nurse and quickly answered the army's call by applying to the Red Cross for admission to the Army Nurse Corps. In addition to her duties caring for patients, she would write letters to a soldier's family letting them know his condition. She felt this would help the soldier heal faster and help reduce the family's anxiety. The federal government's letters and telegrams were typically very brief, causing a family to have more questions than answers. Nurses tended to the physical and psychological wounds of their patients. Smith traveled with the troops on the front lines to provide medical care. She was with the medical unit providing care to the wounded on D-day and at the Battle of the Bulge. During her time in the military, she held positions in hospitals, was a transport nurse and was on the front lines. As a sign of appreciation, soldiers gave their angel of mercy the insignia patch from their uniform. She sewed these patches on the inside lining of her coat. By war's end, there were one hundred patches sewn on it. Each patch was a remembrance of a man she helped care for during a time of crisis.

Lem Cunningham[91] transferred to Camp Forrest from Fort Oglethorpe, Georgia, due to a back injury. It was a logical transfer, since he was originally from nearby Moore County. He was a cook in the Station Hospital for

Above: The Couch family rented rooms to scores of out-of-towners throughout the war, from a few days to a few months. Seated are a few of the boarders. Standing behind them is Mrs. Anabel Couch; her daughter Dot is standing next to her. *Mrs. Dot Couch Watson collection.*

Left: Nurse Paterniti Smith's coat lining had over one hundred insignia patches sewn on it. Each patch represents a wounded soldier she treated. *Judy Jenkins collection.*

approximately three years. Meals were prepared based on the patient's medical condition as per written orders from a dietician. Several POWs worked with the kitchen staff during his employ. Some of the men were quite strong, being able to single-handedly move waist-high barrels of pickles in brine. Cunningham never recounted any incidents or accidents with the prisoners. One prisoner offered to make a carving for him in exchange for a pack of cigarettes. Cunningham supplied the man with the bottom of a cedar nail keg and a small single-edged razor blade. This blade was the only sharp instrument the POW could possess. Each week, the prisoner would ask for a certain color of paint and then a shellac. The finished product was a beautifully carved Indian head with the words "Camp Forrest Prisoner of War" in block letters on the outer rim.

First Lieutenant Rosalind Mokray was a dietician at the POW section of the Station Hospital. She was responsible for planning and ordering special diets for bedridden and ambulatory prisoner patients. The diets prepared ranged from those relevant for ulcer and diabetic cases to soft or fat diets. Dieticians played a critical role during World War II, since they could discern how and what types of foods to prepare to help a soldier regain strength and stamina as quickly as possible. It was important to understand whether a

Staff of the Station Hospital's officers' mess kitchen. Lem Cunningham is located fourth from the left with a hat and apron. *Cunningham family collection.*

Carving created by a German POW in 1943 from a cedar nail keg using a razor blade and paints. The carving was presented to Lem Cunningham. *Cunningham family collection.*

patient needed a higher fat diet or needed to be restricted to liquids. The wrong diet could lengthen the healing process or worsen a patient's condition.

Mamie Brown Brasier held several positions at Camp Forrest. After working in the laundry, she transferred to the medical infirmary at the Station Hospital. Having an LPN license after the war, she obtained a position at Tullahoma's first hospital, Queen City Infirmary. She became an integral part of the organization, ensuring that every patient received the best care possible. As one of the two nurses on staff, she was responsible for assisting the four doctors and tending to patients in the six-bed ward.

Many soldiers at the Station Hospital participated in the Red Cross rehabilitation program "Something for Nothing." The program provided soldiers the opportunity to create articles from metals, leathers, textiles, woods, plastics and Plexiglas. The materials were deemed scraps and donated by local merchants and manufacturing companies. For example, the General Shoe Corporation donated scrap pieces of leather. Soldiers created a variety of goods, such as jewelry, picture frames and lamp bases. The federal government noted the success of the program and incorporated many aspects of it into its army reconditioning program. The occupational therapy programs helped men transition to civilian life or back into military service. The Station Hospital displayed the creations throughout the wards, and several items were on exhibition in Atlanta.[92]

CRIME AND DELINQUENCY

As with any mass arrival of people and implementation of a large-scale military installation, opportunities for civilian crimes ranged from small to large to violent. Base and unit MPs investigated criminal offenses committed by military personnel. Some civilian crimes included price gouging, black market sales, vice, fraud, robbery and murder. According to the Bureau of Labor Statistics, one dollar in the 1940s is the equivalent to approximately sixteen dollars in 2018. It is easy to understand why some citizens may have possessed the impetus to pursue a capitalist mentality given the hardships endured during the Great Depression. In an effort to curtail this behavior, city officials created a board of trade to monitor the supply and pricing of housing rents in the area. In late 1940, Tullahoma mayor Don Campbell hired several additional police officers in anticipation of the increase in criminal activity that typically follows significant population surges. The city built an additional temporary jail facility under the viaduct. Police Chief Frank Wade reported that during the construction phase, arrests increased from forty-five per month to an average of eighty-five per week. However, most of those arrested were able to pay fines quickly by cash.[93] The chief anticipated that this average arrest rate would decrease once soldiers arrived from the military police, who would assist in maintaining law and order on the cantonment. Company E of the Sixth Cavalry from Fort Oglethorpe, Georgia, as well as several FBI agents conducted policing of the base proper throughout the construction phase. Once the base operationalized, the various regimental military police units assumed these responsibilities. Assuming the responsibility of policing a vast construction site as well as Tullahoma would have likely overwhelmed the city's six full-time officers and three reserve officers.[94]

Although there were two banks in Tullahoma, Hardaway Construction payroll account deposits were at the First National Bank. First National Bank president E.D. Blackmon ordered the installation of new revolving front doors and a rear exit door to ensure payroll processing was as efficient as possible.[95] However, on payday, the line outside the bank still wrapped around two city blocks even before it opened. The first construction payday was the end of October 1940. It became common for individuals to wait in line for two to three hours to cash their check.

Enterprising con men took advantage of individuals not interested in waiting in long bank lines by charging a high fee to cash an individual's check instantly. The con man and his muscled bodyguard walked up and down the long line outside the bank, carrying a large sack of cash. He would charge a $5 fee for every $50 of the check's face value. For example, a "customer" with a check valued at $50 would receive $45 in return, but one with a $100 check would receive $90. Although the con man's commission was high, many individuals readily paid it to avoid the long wait. The rate of robbery and homicide also increased at this time of month. Lee Beavers recalled reports of a man found bludgeoned to death by a hammer in the woods outside town, an apparent victim of a robbery gone wrong. Newspaper reports of major offenses, such as prostitution, robbery and murder, became more common in this period. Later reports indicate that police officers and MPs patrolled the areas, especially on paydays, in an effort to maintain law and order.

Engaging in ungentlemanly behaviors defied the commanding general of the U.S. Second Army, Lear's orders, but prostitution arrests and diagnoses of venereal diseases increased. As the first wave of troops arrived in March 1941, city officials and law enforcement began taking steps necessary to eradicate prostitution. Conventional wisdom at the time placed a responsibility on everyone in the community and on base to ensure soldiers were not just physically clean but also morally clean. Mayor Don Campbell reported the problem was curtailed during the construction phase of Camp Forrest because the vice peddlers were prevented from attaining residences. However, prostitutes from Chattanooga, Nashville and other nearby towns became more perceptive and plied their trade in automobiles. Since many soldiers did not leave camp during the week, the instances of flesh peddling occurred most often on the weekends. Camp personnel and citizens stepped up efforts to provide wholesome entertainment for soldiers. However, General Lawton indicated he had authority, if necessary, to declare a building or area out of bounds for soldiers. Any soldier caught in an out-of-bounds area faced severe punishment. Pledged support from various law enforcement agencies would likely forestall the necessity of taking such actions.[96] Should the need arise, soldiers were directed to visit prophylactic stations located within each regiment, as well as ones located at the health clinics in Tullahoma and Winchester. With the implementation of these measures, the federal government hoped to prevent the spread of venereal disease. Many individuals who were elementary school children during this period recalled frequently finding used condoms on the playground, perhaps due to its proximity to the USO building.

The effects of everyone helping prevent prostitution were effective. Base medical officer Captain F.W. Wilson reported that of the 26,000 soldiers stationed at Camp Forrest, only 309 of the men in the prior six-month period had contracted a venereal disease. Officials were able to track the areas where the infections were contracted; only 83 had relations with vice peddlers near Tullahoma. The largest percentage of contagious prostitutes was from the Nashville area and in counties outside the state. Law enforcement traced the 83 cases in the greater Tullahoma area to prostitutes who were plying their trade in taxicabs, private cars or at dance halls and tourist camps. The transient nature of these acts allowed offenders to better evade police detection. Further efforts to eliminate the problem led to the base's medical department distributing weekly reports that indicated the number of infected men within each regiment. Owing to regimental pride, officials believed respective units would increase their own self-policing efforts.[97] In May 1941, Congress passed the May Act, which made prostitution a federal misdemeanor. The punishment for this misdemeanor was a $1,000 fine (approximately $16,000 in 2018), one-year imprisonment or both if acts of prostitution were committed in areas where the federal government had invoked the law. Unlike the previous law enacted during World War I, this one sought to educate soldiers on venereal diseases and to treat both men and women who were infected. Numerous female violators were arrested, prosecuted and jailed for prostitution under the May Act. However, law enforcement did not uniformly administer the act throughout the state. Some towns elected to allow "professionals" to ply their trade to ensure that soldiers had adequate entertainment options and preserve the morality of the town's female population.[98] By May 1942, Secretary of War Henry L. Stimson invoked the May Act for a twenty-seven-county area around Camp Forrest, which accounted for most of the areas within Middle and East Tennessee.[99] Interviews or written accounts of individuals who engaged in prostitution during this period were unavailable. FBI records provided factual details of dates and locations in which acts were committed. Of those records reviewed, only a minimal number of men were prosecuted in comparison to women. Women who were convicted of prostitution were typically sent to the Federal Reformatory for Women in Alderson, West Virginia.

Thefts occurred throughout the cantonment during its operation. Types of theft ranged from small crimes, which included shoplifting in a PX, taking rationed products and bringing contraband onto the base, to larger crimes, including stealing tires and other auto parts. In the motor pool, there was a worker noted for stealing tires. However, one afternoon, the emboldened thief stole a car engine. Others working in the quartermaster division reported contraband, such as alcohol, being smuggled onto base by rail. While soldiers could enjoy beer, the base prohibited the consumption of alcohol.

Although patriotism and southern hospitality pervaded, the criminal element crept into the densely populated areas, in some instances leading to death. In several occurrences, reported robberies turned into murder cases. Individuals were beaten and robbed for their money and possessions and eventually died from their injuries. In February 1941, a passerby found the badly beaten body of Camp Forrest carpenter John Goodson after an apparent robbery attempt went wrong.[100] Some individuals who were children during the war years recounted stories of murders told to them by their parents. Each believed the motive for recounting such tales was to keep them well behaved and ensure they stayed within the confines of family yards and did not wander off. However, one such story ripped from national headlines was the murder of Norma Faye Scogin in May 1943. The assailant, George Johnson, kidnapped her as she returned to her boardinghouse. After riding around the vicinity in a stolen car for several hours, Johnson eventually shot her twice in the chest. The next morning, authorities found her lifeless body buried under leaves and brambles on the outskirts of the Camp Forrest encampment. The assailant shot himself in the head the next day during a police standoff. He died a short time later. Norma Faye's husband, Lieutenant George Scogin, was on training maneuvers when he finally learned the news. Newspapers also reported frequent vehicular deaths, plane crashes, suicides and infant deaths.

Transition to Detention Facility

The Bureau of Immigration and Naturalization designated Camp Forrest as a facility to house aliens and alien immigrants. The first non-naturalized aliens detained were two Germans and an Italian in mid-December 1941. Reports regarded the men as potential enemies of the nation. However, it was never disclosed why they were in the states and why they potentially posed a theat.[101] While the alien immigrant population on base was predominately of German descent, Orala Lelchty[102] recalled seeing numerous male and female Japanese individuals during this period. He did not recall any of the alien immigrants initiating any problems or openly expressing dissatisfaction. The War Department awarded a contract to Rock City Construction to build specific housing units for aliens and alien immigrants. Camp Forrest housed this particular population for less than one year. The government eventually transferred everyone to a facility in North Dakota.

Camp Forrest guard Joseph Lawrence Riggins and guard standing next to German castle replica built by POWs. *Joseph Lawrence Riggins family collection.*

Mr. Boyd's[103] primary job responsibilities at Camp Forrest were to maintain the grounds throughout the facility. Given the shortage of civilian labor, he supervised a POW crew of 100 to 150 men. This crew ensured that the grounds throughout the cantonment were meticulously clean. He did not have significant language barriers, as there was always a translator on the crew. POW crews often worked in their spare time to beautify the compound with rose bushes and flowerbeds. Some men even built beautiful replicas of German castles. Under the direction of Lieutenant Frank Henderick, POWs farmed sixty-eight acres of fruits and vegetables at Camp Forrest. Crops harvested included apples, beets, corn, carrots, cabbage and radishes. These crops helped alleviate food shortages and defray costs of feeding POWs.[104]

Multiple barracks formerly used to house soldiers were converted for use by secretarial pools and administrative divisions so that employees could maintain a work card for each POW being housed at Camp Forrest. Jean Jones[105] had just graduated high school when her typing teacher recommended her for a position on base. After taking the civil service examination, she started work in the finance division maintaining German and Italian POW records. Each record contained information such as the detainee's name, military rank, the camps previously stationed at, work assignments, canteen credits and monies due upon repatriation. Her job was to maintain the records on a daily basis for a certain number of POWs. She fondly remembered carpooling with a friend each day. They would park outside the main gate and ride in the back of a truck to a barrack converted to an office building. She remarked how workers could walk around their respective administrative building and to the canteen during breaks, but they did not have full access to every area on the base. She met her future husband, Clarence, while he trained at the facility. They dated for a year until his division deployed to England and later France. They wrote regularly and married soon after his return to Tennessee.

Louise Pugh[106] was a tall, blond, twenty-two-year-old college student who learned of December 7 listening to the radio with her family in Winchester. Her first job after graduating business college was for the Rent Control Office located in town. This office was important, as it ensured that rents in the area were fair and controlled for apartments, hotels and other types of lodging. In 1943, Pugh started working as a stenographer at Northern Field and eventually transferred to the POW area at the main installation. She was primarily responsible for shorthand dictation for various military staff and interrogators. She delivered the typed letters, notes or records of interrogation to the individual for whom she had recorded the dictation. She carpooled with one of her sisters, who drove a Chevy convertible. The POW trustees who worked as janitors in her office were cordial and respectful. When the camp was decommissioned, the economy in the area suffered due to the elimination of many jobs. Louise Pugh eventually moved to Atlanta to find employment with the Federal Housing Administration. She later relocated to Birmingham, holding positions in the Reconstruction Finance Corporation, the Department of Labor, the Internal Revenue Service and the Occupational Safety and Health Administration (OSHA), completing a period of continuous government service of nearly forty years.

3

GROWING UP IN THE MIDST OF WAR

The lessons and experiences learned during Camp Forrest's short existence had long-lasting effects on the lives of Middle Tennessee's youth. Being so young, many children did not understand the meaning of war, but they helped to "put the ax" to the Axis. Growing up in the shadow of a military base, many youth were unaware that continual disruptions and shortages were abnormal. Many interviewees, who were children during this period, assumed every town in America was filled with soldiers. Many who grew up during this time recall understanding to a certain degree that there was a world war occurring and that the influx of soldiers were going to help win it. Like most children throughout the United States, those in Middle Tennessee learned about the attack on Pearl Harbor on the radio. President Roosevelt's declaration of war brought about a new sense of awareness of world events and the evildoers existing in it. According to the 1940 U.S. Census, there were about 18,522 individuals under the age of nineteen in Coffee and Franklin Counties. This figure soon increased significantly when military families moved to the area. In 1942, the federal government built the East Lincoln Elementary School to accommodate the influx of school-age children. That same year, Tullahoma city officials authorized the[107] hiring of four new elementary school teachers and three teachers for the high school in response to the dramatic increase in school-age children. During that school year, there were fourteen teachers, who taught the 397 students in grades one to eight. The elementary school ran two sessions (morning and afternoon) to accommodate all of the children.

African American students attended Davidson Academy, which was located on South Jackson Street. Professor C.D. Stamps served as the school's principal from 1924 to 1966.[108] Most children attempted to lead ordinary lives and maintain routines, such as attending school, doing chores and having playtime with others.

For younger children, playtime could be a rousing game of hopscotch, jump rope, hide and seek or make-believe war games. Toys were often in short supply, as factories transitioned to war production. Companies that continued manufacturing toys used paper or wood as substitutes, for steel, tin and rubber were deemed critical to the war effort. Toys often had wartime and military themes. Alternatively, homemade toys, such as dolls, provided many hours of entertainment. Reading comics or going to the movies was a wonderful treat. Comics were the preferred reading for children and young adults. At most movies, there was a cartoon, a newsreel and the featured movie. Even the cartoons had war themes and helped children understand world events using their favorite characters. Children helped plant and tend Victory Gardens and participated in salvage drives for scrap rubber, metals, paper, fats and glass; all helped produce war-related products. For example, to produce a life raft required 17 to 100 pounds of rubber and a gas mask required 1.31 pounds. With rubber imports from the Pacific suspended, it was critical to gather these materials from American households. This solution was problematic, as many of the rubber items salvaged were of low quality and unable to create reliable supplies of the aforementioned war-related necessities for soldiers.

While he did not remember broadcasts about Pearl Harbor, as he was only six years old, Johnny Majors[109] learned about the D-day invasion listening to the radio with his grandmother Bessie Bobo. His parents did not talk much about the war, perhaps not wanting to upset their young children (five sons and one daughter). The family lived with grandmother Bessie in Lynchburg. The home they shared had eight rooms and a bath. Bessie lived on one side of the house and the family on the other side. The corner lot allowed for a large Victory Garden in the backyard. As in many homes during the war, a world map hung on the living room wall. Johnny and his grandmother would follow troop movements on the map as they listened to radio broadcasts and read the newspaper. The hardworking, naturally athletic patriarch of the family was Shirley Majors, who was a barber in Tullahoma and Lynchburg. In his spare time, he played numerous sports and officiated the many sporting events held at Camp Forrest. Johnny and his brothers often accompanied their father to work at the barbershop. Whether they watched him cut hair, played in town or attended a movie, the young boys always entertained themselves. Johnny recalls watching his father play basketball, football and baseball. During the war, high school coaches enlisted in the military, which caused school officials to suspend many sports. From their passion for the game, the high school students convinced the principal to allow Shirley Majors to coach them for the season. Although there were no funds in the school's coffers to pay him, the elder Majors accepted the position. Gracious students paid him in-kind with fruits, vegetables and meats. This position led to a long, illustrious career coaching high school and college football.

Johnny, his siblings and their friends spent hours playing war games. Each boy was one of the waring nations. Johnny proudly asserted that he was always the United States, unless there was a mutiny among the players that forced him to be an Axis nation. Christmas gifts of pot helmets and toy guns made the war games more realistic for the boys as they ran through yards and hid behind fence posts and trees. Although his little sister always wanted to play, war games were for boys, at least until mom said otherwise!

Playing on Grandmother Majors's farm with his cousins on one particularly hot summer day, Johnny recalled the scores of trucks, tanks and soldiers marching down the long dusty road. He and his cousins began running soldiers' canteens to the well to refill them with cool, fresh water. After receiving numerous nickels and pennies for their effort, the children decided to form a human chain, quickly passing canteens to and from the well and back to the soldiers. At the end of the day, the group felt like millionaires, as each had a pocket full of pennies.

In comparison to others in the United States, children in Coffee and Franklin Counties had the opportunity to meet people from throughout the United States because of the war and their proximity to Camp Forrest. Joanne Hawkersmith Roberson's family lived at 407 South Jackson Street and rented the bungalow in their backyard to a family from Louisiana whose son was Joanne's age. She remembered numerous fun times playing with him in the backyard. Another family that rented a room from the Hawkersmith family was Jean and Lek Sark. In September 1942, the Sark newlyweds received the news that Lek was to report to Camp Forrest for training. Lek was a member of the 318th Medical Infantry division. Jean was able to obtain a job at one of the base's officers' clubs. Jean lived with the Hawkersmiths for approximately eleven months, from fall 1942 to summer 1943. Jean and the family's matriarch, Christine, became steadfast friends, exchanging Christmas cards for more than six decades. Joanne continued corresponding with the Sarks upon her mother's passing and visited Jean in

Indiana several times. The initial visit marked over sixty years since Jean had seen Joanne, who was a toddler at the time.[110] The people were typically not just boarders in the homes throughout Tullahoma, as some, such as the Sark family, became part of the family, whether participating in Sunday dinners or witnessing precious events, such as a baby's first steps. The times were frightening and often difficult, but people across the nation pulled together to ensure victory both abroad and at home.

A New York couple who rented the smokehouse from the Dean family had never been on a farm and were fascinated with how potatoes grew. Mary Ruth was still in grade school but described how the young woman walked through the potato field with her high heels on.

Dot Couch Watson fondly recalls walking the two blocks to town each day with her grandfather Daddy Billy while pushing her duck in her doll carriage. Throughout the war years, she spent a tremendous amount of time with the tall, white-haired septuagenarian, as her parents and siblings were either working at the store or volunteering in the community to help with the war effort. She learned many lifelong skills under Daddy Billy's tutelage. She learned the fundamentals of gardening as well as how to harvest a variety of fruits and vegetables. They set up a lemonade and vegetable stand in the front yard. She learned the fundamentals of customer service and

A New York couple who rented the smokehouse from the Dean family. The couple had never been on a farm. *Flippo family collection.*

entrepreneurship but had to pay her "wholesale supplier" (aka Daddy Billy) for the supplies. This education and experience may not have occurred if times were different.[111]

Children helped fill a void for homesick soldiers with a single conversation. Some children, such as Glenn Flippo, were able to see war machines up close when soldiers came marching by his parents' farm. Most days, he would "play" war along with the soldiers for the entire day. Although strictly prohibited by army regulations, a solider allowed young Glenn to climb on his tank and took his picture after outfitting him as a "soldier."

Dudley Tipps[112] was only nine years old when he learned of the bombing at Pearl Harbor at school Monday morning. Many of his immediate family members worked at Camp Forrest: his father was at one of the service stations and then the post office; his mother was at the post office; his older brother helped with deconstructing the base; and his older sister worked at the base PXs and canteens. Their family invited numerous soldiers home on the weekends for dinner. Tipps also learned that not many soldiers knew much about farm life. However, everyone found commonalities and enjoyed the camaraderie and conversations. Like many farmers in the area, they hired about ten POWs to help harvest tobacco for two days at his grandmother's farm. None of the POWs could speak English, so the Tippses showed them how to cut the tobacco leaves. Unfortunately, they still cut them incorrectly and generally broke the knives they were using. His grandmother fed everyone lunch while they were at the farm. Even at a young age, Tipps remembered how the POWs very much enjoyed climbing in the high rafters of the tobacco barns.

Growing up in the midst of war had its drawbacks. Teenage hangouts and childhood activities gave way to the needs of the burgeoning military and support personnel at Camp Forrest. It was important that everyone make sacrifices to help win the war. Soldiers besieged many prewar teenage hangouts and activities. Duck's Roller Rink was a very popular haunt for soldiers and teenagers. Estimates suggest that more than four hundred soldiers and civilians attended the rink's grand opening. The facility was open Sunday, Wednesday, Friday and Saturday from 7:00 p.m. to 10:00 p.m. Records or organ music provided the melodies customers skated to. Two other rinks in town opened to accommodate the population influx. James Gist remembers the high school transforming into a "teen town" on Friday nights to give the area's youth a place to go for wholesome entertainment and to help prevent juvenile delinquency. In many parts of the United States, child welfare began to wane as material and human resources focused

Glenn Flippo was only six years old but enjoyed practicing alongside soldiers. Some men outfitted him with rifle, gun belt and canteen. *Flippo family collection.*

Duck's Roller Rink was a very popular haunt for soldiers and teenagers, but it was only open Sunday, Wednesday, Friday and Saturday evenings. *Author's collection.*

more on the war effort. Although the Children's Bureau at the Department of Labor worked to ensure programs were in place for the health, welfare and safety of children, efforts often fell short. Residents worked hard to eliminate the occurrence of these types of problems. Many of Tullahoma's youth began working as soon as possible to help financially support their family and to alleviate the tremendous labor shortages. In his May 1942 address at the National Conference of Social Work in New Orleans, Myron Falk[113] reported that the state of Tennessee experienced a 20 percent decrease in secondary school attendance in the Camp Forrest environs due to labor shortages.

Jeannette Holder[114] was a sixteen-year-old high school student when Camp Forrest activated. She took the civil service exam in her high school typing course because of the shortage of qualified workers. She obtained a position as a bookkeeper for POW records. About seventy bookkeepers worked in the barracks alongside Jeannette. She recalled the rows of tiny desks throughout the barracks that served as workstations. The POWs came into the office area to clean; everyone was always courteous and respectful. Her future husband, Frank, lived on the family farm, which had cows, and they grew corn, soybeans and wheat. They hired numerous POWs throughout the years to help with harvesting. Frank knew most of the men by their first names.

As a Boy Scout, Robert Sanders[115] enjoyed the help with Scouting activities he and others received from soldiers permanently stationed at Camp Forrest. The Sanders family home had three bedrooms, so the family rented the downstairs bedroom. As time progressed and the need for rooms increased, his parents converted the living room and dining room into bedrooms. His father was in construction and often delivered materials during the camp's construction phase. Several times, Robert accompanied him to the site and worked for a short time as a dump truck operator.

Linda Stone Phillips was only three years old when World War II broke out. Her childhood differed significantly from the youthful experiences of others in the Middle Tennessee region. She was stricken with polio and unable to leave her home or have visitors. The polio virus swept throughout the area. By August 1941, Tennessee State epidemiologist Dr. A.E. Hardison reported forty-eight cases of infantile paralysis (i.e., polio) in Coffee and Franklin Counties and another twenty cases in four nearby counties.[116] Numerous children stricken with the virus died; others had to use iron lungs for extended periods. The doctor recommended she be placed on a board, which held her arms and legs straight. The board, built by her father, Herbert Stone, had rollers, which allowed her mother, Raba, to roll her throughout the house as well as the yard. For months, she watched the world go by strapped to the board until the doctor recommended that she have steam baths. A large milk can provided a perfect vessel for the baths, ensuring steam reached her arms and legs. Her mother continually cared for her until she gained strength and was able to walk with the aid of corrective shoes. One sunny day, her mother allowed her to stand in the front yard and watch soldiers passing their home. She still vividly recalls the ground vibrations and sounds of the men marching in unison down the narrowly paved road.[117]

Alberta Parks[118] was a teenager in the war years. During a family trip to Chattanooga, her father gave a soldier a ride. In the course of the ride, the soldier told him the girl in the hit song "I Got a Gal from Kalamazoo" was his girlfriend. The family never knew if that was a true story, but it was certainly fun to think it might be. If true, the young soldier was likely referring to nineteen-year-old Kalamazoo College student Sara Woolley. The male students of Kalamazoo felt Woolley most embodied the characteristics described in the song: beautiful, cheerful, peppy, the toast of Kalamazoo and slightly freckled. The junior sociology major said the title was an honor, and she spent hours promoting Kalamazoo and selling war bonds.

James Shubert[119] was still in high school when the war broke out. He spoke of the emotional devastation of learning a young man from the community was killed in action and how deeply everyone at school was affected. Students and faculty were sympathetic to one another over the losses. The school came together like a large family, providing support when everyone learned former and current classmates were either missing or dead.

James Elkins[120] was still a teenager and, like others in the area, became an entrepreneur. He drove his Model A Ford approximately thirty miles northwest to Shelbyville to buy boxes of candy. Removing the car's back seat enabled him to stack fifty to sixty boxes from floor to ceiling. The nickel candy bars were sold for ten to fifteen cents each to soldiers. James Elkins's future brother-in-law, Howard Powell Jr., remembered it took three hours to learn to ride the bicycle his dad purchased in Shelbyville. This young entrepreneur biked to the Bell Buckle drugstore several times a day to purchase items, such as candy, cigarettes and doughnuts, for soldiers. The men would tip him a couple of dollars each trip. In his haste to deliver soldiers' purchases, there were several crashes along the way. Luckily, young Howard and the merchandise always arrived intact.

Robert Sanders[121] was a high school football player but was enthralled watching his first soccer game. German POWs were unfamiliar with American football. The sport they knew and enjoyed was European football (soccer). One spring afternoon, the Tullahoma High School football team loaded into the backs of several large transport trucks for an exhibition game. Their destination was a large ball field behind the tall, barbed-wire fences. German POWs packed the stands around the field in anticipation of witnessing their first American football game. Throughout the game, "Ooohs" emanated in unison from the stands as the ball flew through the air. Roars of cheering and applause brought the crowd to its feet with each tackle. After the game, the young men were allowed to stay to watch a soccer match. Soccer was a minor sport not played in the South. Therefore, few people were familiar with it. The southerners watched intently as the two teams clad in different shirts took to the field. The teams faced the crowd at attention, and when the command was issued, their arms went up in the air. In unison, *"Seig Heil, Seig Heil"* rang out. Although Sanders knew it was only a German salute, it nevertheless sent chills down his spine that hot spring day.

This experience was not his only interaction with German POWs. Young Robert was often able to play at the Camp Forrest golf course. He would ride his bike early in the morning, so he would have the course to himself. German POWs maintained the course and were often there working early in the morning. On several occasions, Robert's game coincided with the golf course maintenance schedule. The Germans would step back and allow Robert to play through. The encounters were pleasant, and the men smiled at him. It was from these moments that the enemy became human. They had merely been fighting for their country, just as our boys were for America.

4

ENTERTAINING THE TROOPS

Everything from daily radio broadcasts and popular songs to games and movies focused on patriotism and the activities Americans could do to help the war effort. Attempting to entertain a population of seventy thousand was no easy task. But citizens, base officials and various civil organizations made sure there was always something to do or at least somewhere for soldiers to sit to write a letter home. According to Bob Couch, commanders allowed civilians on base to watch movies as well as to attend events and shows at the sports arena. Arena shows featured movie stars and personalities, such as Al Jolson, the New York Rockettes, Walter Pidgeon and Broadway-style camp shows. Sporting events included boxing and wrestling matches, as well as basketball games. Numerous boxing matches featured former Golden Glove champions. There were also dances held.

The sports arena could accommodate eight thousand spectators per event. Given the size of the structure, several events could occur simultaneously. It was common for three events to run at the same time without interfering with one another. Sometimes, sporting events featured professional and amateur athletes as well as soldiers from other divisions and/or camps. Band and orchestra contests pitted musicians from various regiments against one another for top bragging rights. The brass hats felt that having regularly scheduled sporting and entertainment events built morale as well as helped condition soldiers for teamwork.[122] On Monday, April 27, 1942, the world-renowned Fisk Singers, from Nashville's historically black university, appeared in concert at the arena. The concert promoters reserved

"ROCKETTES" AT USO SHOW
CAMP FORREST - 1942
Photo: Couch's - Since 1893

Bob Couch photographed the New York City Rockettes when they entertained the troops at Camp Forrest. *Bob Couch collection.*

seven thousand seats for the event. Admission for the concert was $0.15 for enlisted men (approximately $2.41 in 2018) and $0.25 for officers and civilians (approximately $4.00 in 2018). The proceeds from the ticket sales helped purchase recreational projects and equipment for African American troops stationed at the camp.[123]

Cities within a fifty-mile radius of Camp Forrest set up "Defense Recreational Committees" in an effort to ensure that adequate wholesome activities were available for service members. These committees coordinated with base morale officer Major Willard Haynes. Southern hospitality during these times prevailed throughout the state, as committees worked to find clubs that aligned with soldiers' hobbies and interests, brought girls to dances and ensured theatrical seats were filled for soldier performances.[124]

Radio broadcasts from Camp Forrest were common and featured programs such as *Ask It Ball* and weekly broadcasts from base commanders. Some of the more heartfelt programs sent well wishes from soldiers to the folks back home. The base's 1943 Christmas Eve party broadcasted on

Two base guards stand in front of the sports arena, which hosted numerous concerts and sporting events. *Joseph Lawrence Riggins family collection.*

WSM in Nashville for thirty minutes. The program included a comedy skit, a performance by the WAC Jubilee Choir and several carols sung under the direction of Major Ralph Eades, chief medical examiner.[125] Glenn Miller's *Sunset Serenade* coast-to-coast radio program featured a contest wherein a base would submit the name of a popular Miller tune and the listening public would vote which tune should win. The base that selected the winning tune received a new RCA radio-phonograph player and fifty popular music records. Camp Forrest was the winning base on December 27, 1941.[126]

Mother's Day 1942 was a momentous day at Camp Forrest, as mothers arrived by cars and special trains and buses from Illinois and other states to attend the "Dear Mom" gala celebration. Approximately ten thousand mothers, wives and sweethearts from throughout the United States attended the event. Mrs. W.J. Covington was selected as the Camp Forrest honorary mother from the thousands of applications received from Tennessee mothers. In addition to the large reception, she received a $1,000 war bond, and her son made a special trip from Fort Custer in Michigan for the Sunday, May 10 event. The eighty-eight-year-old mom was serenaded by soldiers singing "That Wonderful Mother of Mine" as she was crowned with a garland of fresh white roses and carnations. Flowers plucked from all of the gardens in surrounding counties ensured each visiting mother would receive a fresh blossom for her special day.

CAMP FORREST
LITTLE THEATRE GROUP

Presents

"GOLDBRICKS AND GOLDBRAID"
- a musical revue in three acts
****
Original script written and directed by
Lt. Charles A. O'Hare
Musical Direction
by
Pvt. Edward Rosenbaum

******

2 43rd C.A. Orchestra under Direction of
Corporal Russ Carlson

****

SPORTS ARENA
CAMP FORREST, TENN.
April 25 and 26, 1944
8:30 P.M.

Program for the play *Goldbricks and Goldbraid*, a musical revue in three acts. Many regiments wrote and produced theatrical products while stationed at Camp Forrest. *Author's collection.*

The day was filled with much pomp and circumstance, as bands played and the events of the day were broadcast locally via WLAC and coast to coast on the Columbia Network.[127] Reports indicate over ten thousand mothers, wives and sweethearts visited that weekend.

Soldiers wrote and produced theatrical plays for the base, and regimental bands played concerts. Many soldiers had radios in their barracks. Some of the more popular radio shows were *The Abbott and Costello Program, Amos 'n' Andy, The Black Castle, Burns and Allen* and *The Great Gildersleeve*. Soldiers inundated town on the weekends, seeking entertainment. Many residents recall there were so many people in town that the sidewalks and streets allowed for individuals only to walk shoulder to shoulder.

As a young college student, Searcy Hopkins enjoyed coming home on the weekends. Many of her college girlfriends begged to come home with her so they too could go to some of the many dances held to entertain soldiers. She fondly remembers the dances held almost every afternoon and evening of the week in town as well as at Camp Forrest. Stripes of ribbon were pinned to a patron's collar so they could leave and return to the dance. Her memorabilia for this period contains dozens of these ribbons. She also served on the Mother's Day court for the celebration held at Camp Forrest in May 1942. After a year at Peabody College in Nashville, she stayed home to help manage the family grocery store, W.J. Couch and Company. The store's butcher and manager, Bill Rainy, was drafted, so Searcy became the new manager.[128] There were relatively few problems with patrons and ration stamps at their N.W. Atlantic Street store. However, one afternoon, a man stopped by the store to pick up a few items but forgot his ration book. While some shopkeepers might have permitted the sale, young Searcy refused to sell the items. Although he promised to return with the coupons, she reminded him that they were required at the time of purchase. The furious patron stormed out of the store. He returned several days later to apologize for his behavior and to commend her for adhering to the rules and for her patriotism.

War bond rallies held regularly in town and on the base resonated as a call to action for civilians to help finance the war. Children and young adults heeded the call to purchase war bonds rather than candy and ice cream. The federal government realized that rallying speeches did not effectively rouse the public to desired calls to action. The approaches to this war had to differ from those used in World War I. The solution was to reach the public via an entertainment medium: the movies. The War Department created a new division, War Films, whose first assignment was to create a series entitled "Why We Fight." The division evolved into the Office of War Information (OWI), with the aim to counter any negative sentiments toward the war. The division worked closely with Hollywood and many of its top directors, such as John Ford and Frank Capra. Between 1942 and 1945, Warner Bros. worked closely with the division to produce approximately five hundred feature-length films, as well as hundreds of shorts and training films with war-related themes. These films promoted one of six morale-boosting themes aimed at increasing Americanism.[129]

On November 3, 1943, base theaters one and two were showing *Lassie Come Home* and *Stork's Holiday*, while theaters three and four were showing *True to Life*, *Figaro and Cleo* and Movietone News. The base received new films almost weekly. The theaters also showed training films during the day when necessary. More than five hundred training films reviewed a variety of military topics. The theaters on base had rough-hewn interiors with wood bench seats. The admission price on base was twenty cents for soldiers and thirty cents for civilians. There were three theaters in Tullahoma: the Strand, the Marshall and Mecca. The Strand and Mecca provided moviegoers additional offerings by showing second-run films. These two theaters mainly accommodated the weekend population surges and were demolished soon after the war ended. The Marshall opened in December 1940 and was located on the north side of Grundy Street between Atlantic and Jackson Street.[130] It contained beautifully appointed art deco interior throughout the lobby and theater. It was open twenty-four hours a day, and many patrons noted it always had ice-cold air-conditioning.

In an effort to avoid weekend crowds, many residents elected to entertain themselves at home. Reading books, playing cards and listening to the radio were top at-home entertainments. Some of the more popular books during World War II were *And Now Tomorrow*, *A Tree Grows in Brooklyn* and

"Be with him at *every* mail call." Individuals were encouraged to write to soldiers frequently to keep morale high. *Northwestern University Library.*

Forever Amber. Sales of the Bible increased approximately 25 percent in the war years. Organizations such as the Red Cross disseminated decks of cards freely to military personnel and civilians. Popular card games included pinochle, gin rummy, poker and hearts.

Uncle Sam continually encouraged Americans to write to GIs. In some instances, letter writers did not know one another but were from the same hometown. Receipt of a letter from anyone kept a soldier's morale high. Some records indicate that receiving letters was second only to eating. The Camp Forrest and Tullahoma post offices processed hundreds of thousands of letters a day. Extra personnel employed during the holiday season ensured soldiers received letters and care packages as quickly as possible. The National Archives Postal Museum found a 1944 survey that indicated 11.5 million service members mailed approximately six letters home per week. Often, service members spent spare time writing home, as postage was free for letters sent to and from military bases. Even in the midst of maneuvers far from civilization, soldiers put pen to paper whenever possible. Many service members subscribed to hometown newspapers and magazines to keep abreast of local news. Letters from family members generally recounted the activities since the last letter sent. For example, Sergeant Robert Cook's[131] letters to his wife, Helen, in Pennsylvania talked about Tennessee's cold February weather and the light dusting of snow on the ground. He recounted the delicious breakfast and his plans to see *Star Spangled Rhythm* by Paramount Studio. As noted in his letter, the movie was indeed star-studded, as actors such as Bing Crosby, Bob Hope, Dick Powell, Paulette Goddard, Dorothy Lamour and Betty Hutton had feature roles in it. The morale-boosting flick received two Academy Award nominations in 1944.

Letters to girlfriends or wives spoke of the lonely soldier's heart's desires or how he and his bunkmates enjoyed the goodies in the recent care package sent. Postcards were typically short hellos to friends and family members. They were sometimes used in lieu of making a phone call to let people know of safe arrival at their destination or where to meet on a specific day. Taylor Drug Store owner Dr. L.E. Taylor sold his entire stock of old postcards within a week of soldiers and their families arriving in the area. The old stock comprised pre– and post–World War I images of the town and businesses. The new stock of postcards depicted any number of town buildings and recreational areas as well as military life and scenes of the cantonment.

5

IT'S THE MILITARY LIFE FOR ME

According to a June 1946 War Department[132] report, Tennessee contributed 2.09 percent of its population to serve in the war. For most of the United States, it was unusual for individuals to travel beyond the borders of their home state, but this would change as soldiers traversed the length of the nation due to the war. Troops and equipment arrived throughout the day and night, as it was routine for troops to receive training from multiple bases before shipping overseas. In November 1943, *Railway Age*[133] magazine reported that "troop movement constitute[d] approximately 19.1% of total railway passenger-miles" and "the average organized troop movement originates somewhere in this country every five minutes, day and night, and every five minutes 150 troops entrain and 150 detrain on American railways." In addition to ensuring efficient and effective movement of troops through the United States, the Traffic Division of the Office of the Chief of Transportation coordinated the movement of equipment.

MILITARY INDUCTION

The induction process consisted of numerous physical and psychiatric examinations. Many men volunteered for service so they could select their desired branch. Although a recruit may have selected his branch of service before the induction process, changes could occur indiscriminately. Such was the case for Wayne Shelton. Although he wanted to enlist in the navy, he recalled the navy recruit chief announcing that "he had filled his quota for the day." The chief stated to the U.S. Marine staff sergeant that the rest of the men in the line would fill his quota as well. With that twist of fate, Shelton became a marine instead of a sailor. During this time, the navy branch consisted of three divisions: Navy, Coast Guard and Marines. After his induction at Camp Forrest, Shelton and the other recruits transferred to San Diego for training. In mid-1945, on his way to the Marshall Islands, Shelton passed through Pearl Harbor. His ship pulled into the harbor near the sunken battleship *Arizona*.[134] It had been four years, but the horrors of the day were still readily apparent. Although the billowing clouds of black smoke were gone, the harbor contained ship debris on the seabed, and the *Arizona* remained capsized. Bullet holes riddled numerous buildings throughout the bases as well as in Honolulu.

Marie Boswell[135] began work at Camp Forrest in February 1942 after making a very high score on the civil service examination. Hired quickly for an induction center administrative position, her primary responsibilities were to interview inductees and process inductee paperwork. Several 4-F soldiers and civilian women worked in that office alongside Marie. (The classification 4-F meant they were not acceptable for service in the armed forces due to medical, dental or other reasons.) Once all of the inductees' paperwork was completed, the local induction boards reviewed everything before making final determinations of fitness. Marie held this position for two years, until the induction center closed on October 1, 1944. She helped process approximately 140,000 men for military duty. Despite the number of inductees processed and the stress of the position, she remarked that there were never any significant problems with the recruits or the examinations. In one instance, a solider mistakenly walked into the administrative office she shared with several other women. Normally, the unexpected walk-in would not have raised eyebrows, but this recruit was clad only in his "birthday suit"! He eventually found the correct office for his physical examination. She also worked in several other administrative positions at Camp Forrest until the war ended. Some of her other administration positions included the Civilian Personnel division interviewing civilians for base employment, the Post Engineering division and the Station Hospital. Unlike other civilian positions at Camp Forrest, none of the administrative positions she held paid overtime. Employees were responsible for ensuring that the work was completed. She recalled long hours at the induction center ensuring the operations continued to run efficiently and effectively.

Once the military determined that a recruit was fit for duty based on the physical and psychological examinations, it was up to local draft boards to determine whether a man was fit for military service. Local draft board fitness considerations included the importance of a man's occupation to the war effort, his health and his family situation. Rollins & Levan Furniture Store manager Bill Hawkersmith was eager to join the military to support his country. His letter from the Office of Naval Officer Procurement indicated that it did not have any openings available based on his background qualifications. His young daughter, Joanne Hawkersmith Roberson, remembered how devastated her father was after receiving his letter.[136]

Once approved by the draft board, inductees were fingerprinted, and they signed their induction paperwork. After assignment to a branch of service, new recruits had a brief furlough before shipping to a training facility, such as Camp Forrest. Additional tests and inoculations and extensive training in multiple areas—including, in part, ordnance, hand-to-hand combat and weapons—followed for several months. The base also had specialized schools for advanced training in areas such as chemical warfare, telecommunications, mechanics and paratrooping. Opportunities in vocational training were also available for various positions and skills, such as clerks, typists, foreign languages and motor mechanics.

During his time during the construction of Camp Forrest, Lee Beavers held positions in the payroll division and as a telephone operator before joining the army in November 1942. After the induction process, he noted how it was different seeing his former place of employment from the soldier's perspective. He felt everything looked great and was proud of the work he had done during the construction phase. After his discharge from the service, Beavers returned to Camp Forrest to help with its dismantling. During his time in the service, he received the Bronze Star for bravery in rescuing civilian firebomb victims in England.

The Fifty-Eighth Signal Battalion trained soldiers to establish telephone and telegraph lines quickly on the front. It was noted that *blitzkrieg* warfare was making communication an integral part of a unit's strategic plan. Soldiers practiced climbing poles and splicing wires during training exercises. The men also practiced using switchboards, using telegraphy keys and learning the army's international code.[137]

Chuck Tyler[138] arrived at Camp Forrest and found the bathrooms in several barracks flooded. He was familiar with plumbing, as he had worked

THE GHOST WALKS

"The ghost walks" was a phrase appropriated for military use. It referred to the doubt someone has regarding whether payday monies are actually distributed. *Author's collection.*

with his master plumber father prior to his military service. In short time, he was able to correct several of the plumbing problems that plagued the base. Overseas, he served with General George Patton's army. He ensured that the plumbing for hospitals and command facilities functioned properly and saw combat in North Africa, Italy and France. He received a Purple Heart for injuries sustained during the Battle of the Bulge.

A notable inductee at Camp Forrest was the second-oldest son of the World War I Tennessee hero Sergeant Alvin York in May 1943. The nineteen-year-old George Edward York was looking forward to becoming an Air Corps gunner. He later received a medical discharge and focused his efforts on being a minister. Many of the soldiers at Camp Forrest had typical names, such as John, William or Robert. However, one young recruit from Chattanooga who presented himself to a recruiting office in February 1941 had a unique name: General Forrest Cope Jr. It was his desire to enlist with the 181st Field Artillery of the National Guard unit so that he could train at Camp Forrest.[139] The *Chicago Tribune* reported in March 1941 that the son of General Samuel T. Lawton, commander of the Illinois 33rd Division at Camp Forrest, would report to the Tennessee encampment by mid-month. Lawton Jr. was only twenty-two years old but had already attained the rank of second lieutenant in the 122nd Field Artillery Regiment.[140]

Harry Pavey[141] and his brother were in the 33rd Division, 208th Field Artillery Battalion. They left Chicago on Saint Patrick's Day 1940. The negative stereotypes of Tennesseans portrayed in films and newsreels were in the forefront of soldiers' and visitors' minds as they traveled south toward Camp Forrest. Residents welcomed the arriving trains, which helped dispel the erroneous preconceived notions out-of-towners might have once held. The base was approximately 95 percent built when the first troops arrived. Amid the sea of mud were a main road of concrete and numerous gravel side roads. Pavey and the rest of the division spent their first two weeks in Tennessee cleaning up the scrapped lumber and tree stumps around the encampment. Once completed, regular military training activities

A shower and shave were important aspects of morning military routine, whether on base or in the field, in order to promote good health. *Author's collection.*

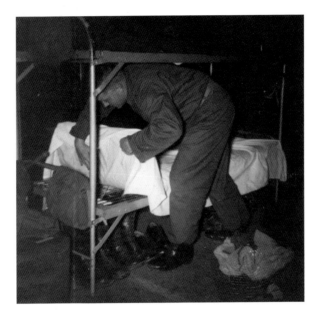

Left: There were no moms, house cleaners or girlfriends to help make beds or change them when the sheets were dirty. *Author's collection.*

Below: Two soldiers review their gear displayed in front of their pup tent. The typical pack that soldiers carried weighed about fifty-four pounds. *Author's collection.*

A rifle was a soldier's good friend. It was important to ensure the rifle was clean so that it fired correctly every time. *Author's collection.*

commenced. On an average day, reveille sounded at 5:00 a.m. and troops dressed, readying themselves for roll call. A quick shower and shave followed roll call. After breakfast, the men engaged in basic, classroom, specialized training and/or hikes for the remainder of the day. Dinner and a short amount of free time completed the day before taps sounded. Marching was part of a division's basic training. During marches, a soldier carried all of his equipment with him. The typical load a soldier carried weighed approximately fifty-four pounds. The typical gear carried included, in part, cartridges and belt (six pounds), gas mask (five pounds), filled canteen and cup (three pounds), half shelter (two pounds), blanket (four pounds), trench tool and carrier (two pounds), rifle (nine pounds) and toilet articles (one pound). Troop marches varied based on command orders and could vary in length and intensity—half day, whole day or multiple days with bivouac. Men had to have the stamina to carry fifty-four pounds of field equipment and traverse great distances. Part of Pavey's basic training was learning to fire large weapons, such as 75-milimeter and 105-milimeter guns, as well as rifles and .45 pistols at Spencer Firing Range. Soldiers leaned to shoot from numerous positions, including prone, sitting, kneeling and standing.

On September 27, 1942, a Memphis father, Jessie Luther Birdsong, and his son, Billy, were sworn into service together at Camp Forrest. On turning nineteen, the son's only birthday wish was to join the military. The World War I veteran not only consented but also decided to enlist. The Birdsong duo left well-paying civilian jobs to answer their nation's call to duty. Each man worked as airplane mechanics at a Memphis war-production plant. They hoped to attain the same type of work and ply their trade side by side. Both men survived the war.[142]

General Patton's headquarters during the Tennessee maneuvers was at Manchester High School. The school still held class throughout the year, but the detached gym became a small PX throughout Patton's "occupation." During the war games "fought" throughout the Middle Tennessee area, you could see Patton riding down Tullahoma's main streets leading his convoy.

REVEILLE, TAPS AND OTHER MUSICAL MELODIES

Tom Jennings's[143] task during the construction phase was putting termite flashing on the buildings. He transferred to the tool and supply room after construction was completed. Although he attended West Point to attain a commission on graduation, he elected to discontinue his studies and enlisted in the National Guard. After learning Uncle Sam needed musicians, he transferred from the army to the 191st Field Artillery Band. Each division had its own band that marched throughout the area playing reveille and taps daily. The commanding officer for Jennings's unit was a Colonel Brown, a retired U.S. Marine noted for keeping the band's tempo with a riding crop. Band companies were the first to rise each morning. The men had to dress and be ready to sound the 6:00 a.m. call. Because they were dressed, they were unable to return to bed for a quick nap before reporting to 8:00 a.m. band practice. The company had the grand idea during the winter months to wear their long peacoats over their pajamas to sound reveille. By rolling their pajama bottoms up slightly, no one would be the wiser. This would allow them to return to warm beds for a bit longer. This minor act of deception worked well for a few days, until a bandmate's pajama leg unrolled below his peacoat. Colonel Brown spotted the infraction and called the company to an immediate halt. He

Reveille played at sunrise, and taps played at sunset. However, it is important to note that many soldiers indicated that their division played these calls at different times of the day. *Author's collection.*

ordered each man to remove his long coat. The men stood at attention in pajamas in the frigid Tennessee morning until they were almost blue before Colonel Brown allowed them to return to their barracks. No one said anything more about the incident. The company did not play reveille in pajamas ever again. In addition to reveille/taps, parades and dances, Jennings's unit played at the Hollywood Canteen. The canteen was a USO-type club located in Hollywood, California. It provided free food and entertainment to all U.S. service members. It differed from other USO clubs, as entertainment industry volunteers staffed it. Service members were able to dance with their favorite starlets. Some accounts suggest that almost three million service members patronized the canteen in its three years of operation. Several times throughout Camp Forrest's operation, members of the Tullahoma High School band had the opportunity to play with the various military bands stationed at the base.

Chow Time

A focus on nutrition in the early twentieth century promoted the consumption of vitamins and minerals in foods and supplements. The virtues of drinking a quart of milk a day were extolled by the medical profession. Improvements to the American diet led to longer lives for many citizens. However, as the war progressed, rationing of food staples became the norm. Posters created by the Office of War Information (OWI) emphasized that well-fed troops would lead to a strong army, which in turn would defeat the Axis. Local farmers grew varieties of crops and sold them to Camp Forrest to feed soldiers. Some of the major crops in the area included corn, beans, wheat, strawberries and tobacco. The cantonment had a canning machine able to preserve one hundred glass jars of vegetables at a time. Canning ensured that fresh fruits and vegetables were available during the winter. Many residents reminisced how soldiers walked up to their homes and asked for home-cooked meals while on maneuvers. Typically, men wanted to eat as many eggs as the farm was able to spare, since it was not feasible to carry them on maneuvers. Families were always happy to cook for the troops. Army policy required soldiers to bury foods they were unable to carry with them. They could not openly give civilians rationed foods. Men were always appreciative for the kindness shown them and "buried" supplies of sugar, coffee and ham in a shallow hole on the property. Once the soldiers left, the family dug everything up.

Many of Private Wesley Slaymaker's letters to his wife chatted about the foods served at mealtime. He indicated that meals were served cafeteria-style and men could sit anywhere in the mess hall. He often remarked how terrible the coffee was, but the milk was plentiful. Local commercial dairies won contracts to supply milk provisions to the base. Many local farmers sold their surplus milk to commercial dairies to help supplement their income. The Cooks and Bakers School was a specialized military school that trained men to properly store and cook foods in the field. The base bakery typically produced thirty-two thousand loaves of bread per day. Reports indicate the quartermaster division for the Fourth Corps Area spent $750,000 (approximately $13,356,602 in 2018) on food supplies for a three-month period in 1941.[144] Sometimes, units had special-occasion meals, such as unit celebration dinners. Some of the menus indicate that these meals featured a variety of meats, vegetables and sandwiches.

Dust and Mud

Many of the construction workers and soldiers would agree with the *Kingsport Times*'s depiction of the muddy and dusty conditions at Camp Forrest. The mud became a quagmire that could sink a man clear up to his knees. On cloudless days, a dusty fog caused by the steady stream of traffic brought flashbacks to the Dust Bowl era of the 1930s.[145] In July 1941, Representative George Bender (R-Ohio) charged that a large number of troops were suffering from "dust bowl throats" and living in misery due to dust inhalation. Major General Lawton, camp commander, denied the accusations, stating that, on their arrival, construction was finishing; once grass began to grow, the problem began mitigating itself.[146] Although only nine paved miles existed when the Thirty-Third Division arrived, by year's end, the fifty-four miles of roads throughout the cantonment were blacktopped.

Allen Wesley Kirby[147] was from Colorado and joined the 168th Battery A Field Artillery division of the National Guard at Fort Collins after completing time in the Civilian Conservation Corps (CCC). It was February 1941 when basic training commenced. A month later, his military convoy left the Colorado mountains destined for those located along the Cumberland Ridge. It took six days to travel the approximately thirteen hundred miles. On its arrival, some of the division's first tasks were clearing debris around the base and making barracks and mess halls habitable. Although the work was not daunting, the area was still very much a mud pit. Basic training followed soon thereafter. In an effort to combat the mud, the War

Interior view of barracks. At the end of the bunk was the soldier's footlocker, which contained all of his personal possessions. *Author's collection.*

Department ordered twenty-six thousand pairs of overshoes. However, Major General Lawton remarked that troops would make the best of the situation until they arrived. The troops would commence the intensive thirteen-week Mobilization Training Program by the end of March 1941.[148] Lawton's program included basic, technical and tactical soldiering. The basic-training program included lessons in military history, soldierly bearing, first aid, hygiene and physical training. Technical programs taught the fundamentals of maps and aerial photography, functions of arms and mechanical equipment and the fundamentals of marksmanship. The final segment, tactical soldiering, prepared men for actual field instruction. In addition to building physical prowess, the program sought to build morale, discipline and alertness in soldiers.

AMERICAN INGENUITY

Salvage drives were a mainstay throughout the war years for both civilians and military installations, since it was difficult to import raw materials during the war years. Preparing salvaged materials for processing was quite time-consuming. Three inventive civilian employees devised an efficient method to bale cardboard. It typically took seven men an entire day to bundle between

Post commander Colonel Frank Addington inspects the new paper baler created by three civilian employees, which helped significantly decrease processing time. *USAHEC.*

ten and twelve bales. During a scrap-metal drive, three would-be inventors devised a contraption that baled approximately ten bales of cardboard every four hours by using only four men.

Another instance of American ingenuity occurred at Camp Forrest in June 1941. Lieutenant Charles Yancy and Captain Lowell Bean improved the army's $640 anti-tank gun for only $6.38. With U.S. soldiers saving money and developing alternative solutions in the field, many lives were saved and the war concluded more quickly. Conversely, reports from the front indicated that German soldiers would typically send a weapon or vehicle back to a manufacturing plant for repair rather than attempt to make a simple repair themselves.[149]

Second Army Ranger School

After the disappointing performance of the Red and Blue Army commanders during the Louisiana maneuvers, Lieutenant General Ben Lear conceived of establishing a Ranger school. Working with numerous other commanding officers, the leader of the U.S. Second Army foresaw the need for a specialized training school that would prepare select military leaders in the "art of killing." By the fall of 1942, the Second Army Ranger School course of instruction had been completed and the invitations to a select cadre of soldiers to participate were distributed. The subject schedule manual for the Camp Forrest Second Army Ranger School indicated that qualifications of the individuals who were selected for this division were based, in part, on their "qualities of leadership, for [their] outstanding physical fitness to ensure the hardship of combat and for [their] personal ingenuity." The manual also stated that the enemy comprised "outlaws, dastards, and fanatic military maniacs." The Second Army Ranger School was America's answer to total war. In January 1943, the seven hundred soldiers selected began two weeks of intensive training that stressed the development of physical, mental and overall stamina as well as coordination as a team. The course of instruction included:

1. *Physical conditioning, which was twenty-one hours of lectures and training on proper techniques of physical conditioning*
2. *Hand-to-hand combat, which included eight hours, wherein the soldier learned to defend himself with and without weapons. Without-weapon instruction focused on dirty fighting techniques.*
3. *Individual camouflage training consisted of six hours explaining how to utilize available resources to disguise one's self and weapon. It also provided students with an understanding of the techniques the enemy used to discern troop movements, locations and strategic sites.*
4. *The wire entanglements course was an eight-hour course that taught the soldier the basic construction of obstacles, how to deconstruct them and the various types of entanglements employed. The typical entanglement utilized was barbed wire.*
5. *Sniping and infiltration was a six-hour course, which taught effective use of firing various types of guns in an effort to maximize damage to enemy troops.*
6. *Patrols and ambush training provided soldiers with proper techniques of aggressive patrolling and dealing with potential ambush situations. Practical skill lessons included learning various sounds, smells and lights at night.*

7. *Stalking and ambushing tanks taught "tank hunting skills" in the ten-hour course of instruction. Soldiers learned tactical tips and best practices, as well as the basics of creating grenades and mines, and ambush and attack techniques during the day and night.*

8. *Stream crossing expedients and use of toggle ropes was a six-hour course that taught the ranger how to create various mechanisms to cross a stream or river. Some of the methods covered included flotation, aerial cableway and toggle rope bridges. After each demonstration session, rangers practiced the techniques observed.*

9. *The Combat Reaction Proficiency course helped hone soldiers' skills and aggressiveness in the use of weapons. It further helped instill self-confidence, speed and coordination of soldiers' thoughts and actions. The proficiency course contained a blitz-bayonet course. The second part of the course simulated real-life ambushes as the soldier completed the course. The techniques of mountain climbing and repelling were practiced. Rangers also trained in a mock German village in an effort to familiarize themselves with the warlike sights and sounds they would soon encounter on the front. The men who graduated from this course were pivotal in the D-Day invasion, storming the beaches of and scaling the cliffs at Normandy.*

Minority Units

African Americans answered Uncle Sam's call to action at home and abroad. African Americans' fight for victory was momentous, as these men and women chose to go to war in the hopes of ending tyranny and oppression not just abroad but also on the home front. Racism and discrimination at home were prolific during this period. Although President Roosevelt's Executive Order 8802 prohibited discriminatory employment practices in national defense industries, the practice continued unabated until labor shortages forced employers to hire all able-bodied workers. A fire destroyed Camp Forrest's enlisted personnel records, so an accurate account of the African American personnel stationed there during its operation is unavailable. However, research indicates these were some of the African American divisions trained at Camp Forrest:

28th Quartermaster Regiment
6888th Central Postal Directory Battalion
98th Engineer Battalion
184th Field Artillery
24th IM Car Company
580th Ordnance Company
365th Engineering Battalion
65th Quartermaster Battalion
366th Engineering Company

Newspaper stories, government documents and interviews provide details and a better understanding of the African American experience at Camp Forrest. Many accounts indicate that morale was low, as African American service members lived in separate areas of the encampment. The base was a segregated facility. Their accommodations and recreational amenities were substandard or nonexistent in comparison to other facilities in the

An African American detachment drilling at Camp Forrest on September 22, 1941. Specific details on the battalion or the soldiers is unknown. *NARA-CP.*

Left: Military desegregation did not occur until 1948. African American soldiers lived and trained in separate, but not equal, sections of the cantonment. *Author's collection.*

Below: African American soldiers from one of the numerous Infantry and Tank Destroyer Battalions stationed at Camp Forrest in front of the Headquarters Building *Author's collection.*

encampment.[150] Several interviewees indicated that there were minimal race relations among Tullahoma's citizens in this period. However, racial tensions and problems persisted on the base.

The military did not desegregate until after President Harry Truman issued Executive Order 9981 in July 1948. Over one million African Americans served in World War II. Relegated to mainly menial support roles, African American male soldiers served as cooks, janitors, post office workers and drivers. Many African American enlistees were dubbed untrainable, slow to react and fearful of combat. However, over one million black service members proved these claims patently false. Subjected to Jim Crow transportation practices, service members were required to sit in the back of the bus and could board only using rear doors, even if they were in their military uniforms. Many soldiers returning to the United States from the front endured worse treatment than did German POWs detained on the same soil. Little documentation exists regarding training, service and treatment of African Americans at Camp Forrest. The few surviving documents indicate that treatment and resources were second-rate. Several memos sent from Lieutenant Colonel Marcus Ray, commander of the 600nd Field Artillery, 92nd Division, to Truman Gibson, civilian aide to Secretary of War Henry Stimson, indicate that various commanders would not allow the library, PXs nor individuals to subscribe to African American newspapers, such as the *Pittsburg Current* (Pennsylvania) or the *Chicago Defender*. These papers were considered contraband; soldiers who subscribed to them were at risk of repercussions from base MPs. The War Department eventually issued an order by the end of 1943 that base commanders did not have authorization to decide which publications would be available at a military installation. The War Department was the only entity empowered to make those decisions.

Many African American soldiers resisted the Jim Crow norms of the day.[151] Sometimes, not adhering to the norms resulted in repercussions from superiors or MPs. However, some reported "infractions" did not result in disciplinary actions. One incident that escalated unnecessarily resulted when the base commander forced African American troops to leave one of the theaters because they were sitting in a nonsegregated section. They refused to leave the theater, and MPs armed with machine guns arrived and commanded the soldiers to leave the area immediately. The base commander was relieved from duty because of his authorization to use extreme force. Little improvements in conditions and treatment occurred when the new base commander took over. Within the segregated section of the cantonment, there was no library, and the recreation hall and the PX were inadequate compared to the nonsegregated facilities. Transportation was difficult to secure, as Jim Crow norms prevented African American soldiers from obtaining train or bus tickets in a timely fashion for day trips or furloughs. If a soldier was able to obtain a ticket, the segregated train cars were typically subpar or were a freight car.

While morale was low due to the continual insurmountable obstacles, African American service members felt that the fight for Double Victory was worth it. The slogans "V for Victory" transformed into the "Double V" movement when the weekly African American newspaper *Pittsburg Courier* printed James Thompson's letter to the editor. In his impassioned letter, Thompson spoke of his willingness to fight and die for the nation he loved, America. Moreover, as a twenty-six-year-old man of color, it was unjust to ask him to live as half an American if he was willing to offer a full measure of devotion to the cause. He had faith that America would one day become the nation he envisioned, but African Americans must adopt the "Double V" as a reminder to fight for victory over aggression, slavery and tyranny both abroad and at home. His letter became a rallying cry for African Americans throughout the United States.[152]

World War II brought about an unprecedented number of opportunities for women. The federal government encouraged women to enter the workforce to fill positions vacated by soldiers. Many women joined the military out of a sense of patriotism and a desire for adventure. Portrayals of World War II female military service members in movies and newsreels were generally inaccurate. However, it did not stop the more than 350,000 women from joining. In mid-1943, President Roosevelt signed a law establishing the Women's Army Auxillary Corps (WAAC), but it was not until the persistence of First Lady Eleanor Roosevelt and civil rights leader Mary McLeod Bethune that African American women could enlist. Approximately 6,500 African American WAACs served in World War II.

Although many African American WACs had either college or trade school training, they were assigned manual labor tasks, such as scrubbing floors or pushing food carts through the hospital. In several reported instances of physical assault, the NAACP called for the War Department to take action at Camp Forrest. In one instance, white paratroopers attacked African American WAACs in their barracks during the night. While the attack was scary and emotionally disturbing, there were no reports of major injuries to the women. Guards were posted outside their barracks twenty-four hours a day to ensure no further attacks occurred. Base commanders also deemed the area off limits to all white service members. In another instance, white paratroopers dragged African American soldiers into the woods. WAACs followed in pursuit with makeshift weapons but were unable to locate the victims or the attackers. No further reports regarding the injuries and outcomes are available for this particular attack.

Segregationist mentalities pervaded throughout not only society but also the military. Dorothy Thelma May Miller recalled numerous discriminatory instances during a 2001 interview for the Women Veterans Historical Collection. She joined the Women's Army Auxiliary Corps in February 1943. During this period, African American recruits were assigned to a division referred to as WAAC Detachment Section Two. White recruits were assigned to WAAC Detachment Section One. After basic training, Dorothy was transferred to Camp Forrest. She was assigned to work at the Station Hospital at the eye, ear, nose and throat operating room. Although she trained as a librarian during basic training, she became a medical technician at Camp Forrest. As a medical technician, she assisted with surgeries and sterilization of equipment. Her division received a citation as one of the best medical detachments at the encampment. Although the base had a laundry facility, Miller recalled that a white WAC stopped by her barracks to ask if anyone there wanted to do laundry and quality ironing. Miller quickly replied, "No, we don't know of anyone, but if you find someone, let us know because we need someone to do ours." Nothing else came of the incident, and no one else ever approached these recruits regarding laundry services. There were good times attending the service clubs, watching movies and taking the train to Atlanta for long weekend visits. Miller retold of a time when the young group of African American WACs attended an Iowa church; the parishioners welcomed all of them and took them home for dinner. It was a wonderful day, as the women did not have to fight the daily double prejudice due to their gender and race.[153]

Many African American women were already serving in medical detachments in the armed services when the 6888th Central Postal Directory Battalion activated. The 6888th was an all-black battalion of the Women's Army Corps stationed at Camp Forrest. The 855 WACS— 824 enlisted women and 31 officers—comprised women from various geographic regions, educational backgrounds and socioeconomic statuses. The battalion did not receive support services, such as chaplains, motor pool and cooks, from other divisions, so it set up its own infrastructure. Although a majority of the battalion's members served as postal clerks,

Dorothy M. Miller (*far right*) poses with two fellow African American WAACs. *Women Veterans Historical Project, University of North Carolina at Greensboro, University Libraries.*

their female infrastructure comprised mechanics, cooks, chaplains and beauticians. The battalion was required to complete basic training, just like Uncle Sam's other nieces and nephews.

Mail delivery and distribution overseas were not as efficient as the postal services on the homefront. A backlog of letters and packages sent to the European Theater of Operations (ETO) began to fill aircraft hangers. The WACs shipped out for England in February 1945. Commanders anticipated it would take at least six months to eliminate the backlog of mail in Birmingham. The 6888th stayed true to their motto, "No mail, low morale," and completed the task in three months. The battalion worked three eight-hour shifts, seven days a week amid the extremely poor working conditions. The aircraft hangar was unheated, and the blacked-out windows made lighting conditions within the facility poor. They devised a system to ensure that mail for soldiers with a common name received the correct letters. They were also able to clear the backlog of undeliverable mail, forwarding them to

Above: Some of the women of the 6888th Postal Battalion, the all-black battalion of the Women's Army Corps. *Author's collection.*

Right: Essie Woods in front of Camp Forrest barracks. African American women endured significant hardships serving their country, from verbal insults to physical assaults. *Author's collection.*

the facility in record time. The battalion was transferred to Roven and Paris, France, and was able to reduce the reportedly several years old backlog of mail. Again, the backlog cleared in significantly less time than anticipated.[154] Interviews conducted in 1997 for *To Serve My Country, to Serve My Race* speak of the patriotism and sense of duty these women felt amid racial and gender discrimination. One such patriotic member of this battalion was Augusta, Georgia native Essie O'Bryant Woods. She and her two sisters joined the armed services in May 1943. The sisters received initial training at the officer training school for women at Fort Des Moines in Iowa. Essie transferred to a medical unit at Camp Forrest's hospital, maintaining medical records. She and her sister Tessie eventually transferred to the 6888th and served overseas together. When asked about her time in the service, she remarked that it was one of the best times of her life. Not only did she help her nation win a war, but she also was able to visit and explore many of the wonderful cities in England and France.

SOMEWHERE IN MIDDLE TENNESSEE: LET THE WAR GAMES COMMENCE

War games fought throughout the Middle Tennessee region exposed soldiers to the possibilities of as many real-life horrors of war as possible. Part of basic training also included participation in lecture series. Soldiers were required to attend three lectures a week for thirteen weeks to learn about history, geography and current events. The program's purpose was to help soldiers understand the expectations of them in the field. The Second Army commander, General Lear, threw away the textbooks when it came to training his troops to fight hand-to-hand and in combat situations. Every aspect of the "final exam" mirrored reality based on combat reports and talking with returning soldiers. The realistic simulations of the homefront experience could lessen the horrific reality of the front, allowing better and quicker decision making and less loss of lives, as well as a shorter war. Soldiers learned practical fighting strategies and tactics.

It was important to ameliorate as much fear and stress that the actual overseas battle conditions could induce. By the end of the war games, troops would be accustomed to the sights, sounds and smells of war. Spencer Artillery Range was a 30,617-acre heavy artillery firing range that allowed soldiers to practice using large artillery weapons. The Second Ranger

Battalion practiced rappelling and bluff-scaling on the Rocky River Gulf on the Camp Forrest annex. The men who practiced on these cliffs were some of the first soldiers to storm the beaches of Normandy and scale its ninety-foot bluffs. With the practice in Middle Tennessee, the elite squadron scaled the Normandy cliffs quickly amid continual gunfire. Soldiers practiced constructing and blowing up bridges in the area. Being able to construct or reconstruct a destroyed bridge overseas would ensure troops stayed on course and arrived at their destination on time.

Eva Jean Hildman[155] recalled vividly an extremely hot and humid summer afternoon when several soldiers fell down in exhaustion on the hard, dusty Tennessee clay road in front of the laundry. She rushed to aid the men with cool water, but the unit's commanding officer immediately sternly admonished her for her actions. The bellowing voice instructed her to take the water away immediately. She waited until the commander was out of sight before returning to ensure each man had some cool water to help revive him. While she understood and was commanded to leave the area, her compassion and decency overruled the directive. Also concerning overruling directives, William Goddard[156] spoke of several instances when soldiers found illegal stills and ran into moonshiners while on maneuvers in the woods. During one such encounter with an old shiner, the man accused Goddard of being a revenuer. As government employees charged with the destruction of illegal alcohol operations and with orders to arrest anyone caught in the production or sale of the illegal elixirs, a revenuer was an unwelcome sight. Being a young man from the great state of Tennessee, he replied quickly and gruffly that he was a soldier and most certainly not a revenuer. The moonshiner brought a corncob-corked jug filled with the white elixir as a peace offering. Although consuming hard liquor was against army regulations, Goddard took a swig from the jug to prove his tale to the old shiner and ensure his safe escape. At that time, checking out a shiner's still in the woods could get a person shot.

Men from various regions of the United States trained at Camp Forrest. Distinct regional perspectives and norms were readily evident among the troops. There were several instances of soldiers from big cities chased by bulls, as they were unaware that climbing into a bullpen was quite harmful to life and limb. William Goddard was one of the first individuals drafted in Memphis. After a short stint at Fort Oglethorpe, Georgia, he transferred to Camp Forrest. He and his men spent a day pulling their howitzer to Spencer, Tennessee, which was approximately fifty miles from base. The 165-man battalion spent ten months in a tent city in the fields outside of Spencer.

Pon. Bridge Across Cumberland River

Bridge building was an important tactical skill for soldiers to learn. Whenever crossing a river was necessary, the Corps of Engineers could build a pontoon bridge. *Author's collection.*

Infantry Crosses a Bridge on Murfreesboro-Lebanon Road

The number of miles marched daily depended on weather, destination and anticipated arrival date and time. A division could easily cover fifteen miles per day. *Author's collection.*

Left and opposite, top: Whether on base or in the field, the shower and shave were part of the morning routine. Hygiene was an important component of military life. Matters of health and hygiene became important aspects of society after the influenza epidemic took the lives of approximately 500,000 Americans. *Author's collection.*

The government owned the property on which soldiers established their encampment, but local farmers often appropriated the fields for raising pigs. The soldiers did not run the pigs off the land but, rather, lived among them. As was the case most mornings, Goddard's tent mate, Davidson, had a hard time waking up. After several mornings, the soldier's routine garnered the attention of the unit's commanding officer, a Colonel Flutter. The colonel told Goddard it was now his responsibility to ensure that Davidson was awake and reported for duty on time. The next morning, he woke Davidson and made sure he was sitting upright on the bedside before heading to the latrine to wash up and dress. On his return, he saw that Davidson had fallen fast asleep. Since cold, wet washcloths were unavailable, Goddard stuck his head out of the tent and hollered, "Whoo pig pig," and instantly, the tent filled with what seemed like one hundred pigs. Davidson did not need help waking up on time in the future.

Coffee County native Marion Bell recalled instances when his urban comrades were exposed to the trappings of rural life. Having never seen a cow, one New York soldier immediately wanted to know what type of animal

This Walter Hill, Tenn. Wagon Maker is too Busy to Watch the Maneuvers

Maneuvers occurred throughout the day and night, but people carried on with normal daily routines, allowing the war to play out around them. *Author's collection.*

was standing in the field. Bell asked the soldier if he'd ever had milk, and the soldier said, of course. "Well, those are cows, and that's where milk comes from." The solider replied that he would never drink milk again! Another New Yorker proudly showed everyone a set of rattlesnake rattles. When asked how he obtained them, he boasted he got them off a "big worm"![157]

One of the largest divisions at Camp Forrest was the Thirty-Third Illinois Division, whose soldiers were from Greater Chicago and its environs. However, several soldiers from other states were also assigned to this unit. One such soldier was native Tullahoman Leslie Clifton. The army drafted Clifton in February 1942. Most of the men in his outfit were born and raised in larger northern cities like Chicago. These men were generally unfamiliar with the trappings of a rural southern upbringing. While he got along well with his fellow soldiers, their commonalities were few. Clifton recounted[158] to his son-in-law Joel Muehlhausen and journalist Weldon Payne an incident in Bougainville, New Guinea, when it was good to see someone else from the South. Clifton helped cut mahogany trees on the island to construct barracks and mess halls for the troops. Chainsaws were unavailable, so the crew's only option was to use a two-man crosscut saw. Crosscut saws could range in size from four feet to twelve feet in length. Pushing and pulling the thin blade of the crosscut saw could become an arduous task for the stoutest soldier. It was no surprise to Clifton that his northern compatriots were unfamiliar with using the saw. He recalled:

> I'd thought all along I was the only rebel among all the yanks in the entire 129th Infantry. Boy was I surprised the day I saw this old boy pulling a crosscut like it was a toy. I said, "Hey, where are you from?" He answered with the name of his outfit. No, I replied, I mean where are you "from"? He stopped pulling the cross cut, wiped his sleeve across his face and said "Alabama, why?" I knew it, I said. It felt really good having somebody on the other end of the cross cut saw who knew how to pull it.

6

WARTIME HOUSEHOLDS

I t was an extraordinary time, when an entire nation devoted efforts and made sacrifices for over three years and eight months to help win a war raging on the other side of the world. A vast support system on the home front was critical to ensure victory and the return of men and women fighting for freedom. Wartime homes in the Middle Tennessee region differed based on location: town versus rural areas. Houses in midsized cities typically had running water, indoor plumbing and electricity, whereas those in rural areas tended to not have these basic amenities prior to World War II. Homes in rural areas were typically farms, so responsibilities involved caring for farm animals, preparing and harvesting crops, farm upkeep and selling excess food supplies. Water in rural areas came from wells and was carried by buckets into homes. Families kept perishable foods cold using ice or by lowering them into wells when electric refrigeration was unavailable. The Tullahoma Ice and Coal Company delivered ice to residents, which allowed them to keep foods cold. Alan Gray remembered that his grandparents' family icebox used a block of ice to maintain cold temperatures. A small sign placed in the home's window indicated to the ice delivery person how many pounds to leave. Glenn Flippo[159] indicated that his family buried the block of ice under sawdust, which prevented it from melting quickly in the summer. Electricity transformed a nation once constrained by the rising and setting of the sun. The modernization of homes via electricity made them cleaner and safer and provided greater illumination. The addition of appliances to electrified homes, such as the refrigerator and washing machine, allowed household chores to be completed more quickly, which provided families, especially homemakers, more free time. Several women who grew up on farms in this period remembered their mothers making dresses from flour and feed sacks. The practice started in the Great Depression, when families had to make do with the materials they had on hand. The practice continued unabated given the shortages during the war. A commonality many homes throughout the area shared was hanging service flags in the front window. The blue stars on the flag symbolized the number of children serving in the military, and gold stars symbolized a life the family had lost due to the war. Unfortunately, there were numerous homes in Tullahoma and the surrounding areas that hung gold-starred flags in their windows.

BUSINESS AS UNUSUAL

Many of the participants in this oral history project discussed in retrospect that their families were extremely poor in the 1940s. However, at the time, they were unaware of their poverty, as there was a roof over their heads, food to eat and clothes to wear. They typically did not want for anything else. However, in those instances when times and funds became scarce, many businesses throughout Tullahoma ensured that citizens did not starve. One such business was W.L. Couch and Sons. Founded in December 1893, W.L. Couch and Sons was one of the area's prominent general stores. Although the Depression hit the area hard, Daddy Billy, as everyone knew him, was always concerned with ensuring that individuals and families did not go hungry. Whether by barter, trade or temporarily working for the store, customers were loyal and ensured debts were eventually paid. Grandson Bob recalled that a young man temporarily traded his goat for a pair of shoes and some food. The young man eventually paid his tab with the store but elected to leave the goat in Daddy Billy's care. The goat ultimately became a family pet.

To this end, many residents attempted to maintain their prewar activities and traditions in the Camp Forrest years. However, residents adjusted and adapted with the influx of people and war-related lifestyle changes. War-associated changes included blackouts, rationing and labor shortages. Blackouts were a regular occurrence in Tullahoma, even though it was nine hundred miles from the East Coast. Homes and businesses were required to cover windows with heavy curtains or heavy cardboard or to paint them, to ensure that light or reflections did not emanate from the building. Once the sirens sounded the blackout warning, everyone was required to go inside and make sure there were no lights turned on or visible from the outside. Driving at night became risky, as drivers were prohibited from using their vehicle's headlights. Vehicle-related accidents increased significantly due to the inability to see approaching objects. Both of these measures were important to the war effort, ensuring potential enemy aircraft flying overhead could not identify and bomb the town. Camp Forrest was also subject to blackouts. Soldiers who were clerks had to learn how to type in these conditions.[160]

Mary Talley[161] recalled one such drill, when she and her family huddled in the darkness around the radio listening to war reports. The dim light from the radio was visible, causing the air raid warden to reprimand the family for noncompliance. Hal Broyles was in his early teens when the war began, but he recalled the air raid drills in detail, as practices occurred every Sunday. His father, a warden for the street on which they lived, patrolled the streets during each two-hour practice session. Hal was glad when the all-clear signal was issued, as he could go outside to play with his friends.[162] Alan Gray recalled several stories of relatives who owned businesses downtown who painted windows to ensure light did not reflect off the windows. By December 20, 1941, a draft of a proposed air-raid warning system for Tullahoma and Camp Forrest was under review by the War Department. In the proposal, given the distance from the U.S. coastlines, the military would not trigger any alarms unless enemy aircraft were flying toward the Middle Tennessee area.

Another lifestyle change particular to Tullahoma was the restriction on being able to easily cross the street. As a teenager, Mary Talley and her friends would walk to town, but on numerous occasions, it became an ordeal to do so. There were steady streams of military cars and trucks passing through town on maneuvers. Many of the military vehicles included armored combat cars with machine guns, motorcycles, field ambulances, personnel carriers, jeeps, supply trucks and various tanks. One day, she and her friends counted 150 vehicles that passed them before they were able to cross the street. Parents kept watchful eyes on younger children for fear a passing car would accidently hit the youngsters. Road congestion outside of town reduced significantly with the construction of military-only roads to cities such as Nashville, Manchester, Winchester and Shelbyville. Civilians were prohibited from using these new highways. After the war, many of the roads were opened for civilian use.

Rationing

Having lived through the Depression, many residents were already accustomed to being frugal. Wartime kitchens still created healthy and delicious meals despite rationing and shortages. The rationing of staples such as sugar, coffee and butter required women to adapt their prewar recipes. The federal government and food manufacturers published recipe booklets designed to help women prepare satisfying alternative family meals. Many families would invite soldiers to join them for a home-cooked meal and camaraderie, although food shortages were possible. The military did not provide supplies nor reimburse families for these random acts of kindness. These small gestures helped boost everyone's morale.

Food rationing helped ensure that soldiers had enough to eat. The Office of War Information (OWI) created posters touting that well-fed armies were stronger and could potentially defeat the enemy faster. In some instances, rationed products were also used as a component in producing war goods. The Office of Price Administration (OPA) enacted sugar rationing by spring 1942. With sugar supplies cut off from the Philippines and Hawaii, U.S. supplies would deplete quickly without rationing. Sugar cane was a component in the production of gunpowder, dynamite and other chemical products. Butter required a significant number of ration points to purchase, so manufacturers created oleomargarine as a substitute. The oleomargarine came in a pouch and was white in color. Kneading the packet of yellow and red food coloring provided with each purchase made the margarine look similar to butter. Dot Couch Watson remembered numerous occasions as a child kneading the food coloring in margarine in an effort to give it a butter-like appearance. The American Fat Salvage Committee urged citizens to save fats rendered from cooking. A pound of fat contained enough glycerin to create a pound of explosives. Fresh fruits were difficult to obtain, and citizens were required to turn in the tin toothpaste tube in order to obtain a new tube. Tin was in short supply given the war, so every effort was made to conserve precious metals.

In addition to food rationing, the OPA instituted shoe, vehicle tire and gasoline rationing. Most civilians were limited to only three new pairs of shoes per year. However, as the war continued, the limit decreased to two pairs annually. To ensure compliance, a ration coupon was necessary at the time of purchase. However, some citizens obtained products via black markets or used counterfeit ration books. Fashionable footwear was a luxury, and the federal government limited the type and style of shoes available to the public. It was necessary for much of the dwindling supply of leather to be devoted to the war effort. Many shoe stores would run ads in local newspapers announcing when a new shipment was slated to arrive. Dwight Stubblefield worked at the Clayton Shoe Company in downtown Tullahoma and recalled how crazy life became with the arrival of a shipment. To control crowds, the clerks would allow the maximum capacity of customers in the store and then lock the doors. Once everyone completed their purchases, another group was allowed in and the doors locked again. The process was repeated until all the shoes were sold or the last customer helped.[163]

Gasoline rationing began in May 1942 and was supervised though the use of stickers placed on a vehicle's windshield. Sticker types indicated the purpose of the vehicle and the amount of gasoline the owner could purchase weekly. The most common sticker issued to the public was "A." The "B" sticker was primarily distributed to business owners, where as the "C" was for specific professions, such as doctors, nurses, ministers or construction workers. Sticker recipients had to attest that they owned no more than five tires per vehicle. Enforcement of the "Victory Speed" speed limit of thirty-five miles per hour was an effort to conserve gasoline and reduce wear on tires. Tires in this era could puncture easily and wear out quickly. Owners became adept at continually patching and re-patching tires, as purchasing new ones was difficult and costly. Glenn Flippo and Robert Dean recalled often watching family members patch tires with products such as Camel Vulcanizing Patches.

Property Damages and Labor Shortages

Although city and farm life differed, rolling tanks and marching soldiers were common sights. Troops and tanks were not concerned if their battle took them through a farm, a crop or a city street. The army paid for damages caused during maneuvers. Glenn Flippo's family received cash and fencing supplies for damages to their farm. Sometimes, recompense requests went directly to the War Department, but there were occasions when an individual followed the troops and paid the owner for damages on the spot.

Many families, both in town and on farms, planted personal gardens due to food shortages and to ensure there were enough food supplies for troops. Victory Gardens were an important part of homefront life. The family garden became a mainstay as the war progressed. Each Victory Garden

Soldiers in a tobacco field while on maneuvers. Soldiers dug trenches and foxholes or cleared the area of enemy combatants whenever and wherever it was necessary. *Author's collection.*

allowed commercially grown produce to be sent to military installations and overseas to feed the troops. Estimates indicate there were approximately twenty million Victory Gardens throughout the United States. These gardens supplemented approximately 40 percent of the nation's vegetable consumption. Many homes preserved extra produce grown by canning. Families had "fresh" produce available in the winter months, and other items could be purchased with ration points. James Shubert[164] was in his early teens during the war, but he recalled that the big family garden received a World War II Victory Garden Award for being one of the area's best gardens.

Despite the war preparations and the arrival of POWs to the area, most families maintained their adjusted daily routines and kept as many prewar traditions alive as possible. Churches throughout town were important havens for social and recreational activities for civilians and military personnel. Volunteers were on hand throughout the days and evenings to ensure adequate resources were continually available for military personnel. The First Baptist Church of Tullahoma,[165] along with help from the Baptist State Board, established a service center and a soldier's lounge and served refreshments in the kitchen. Church reports and meeting minutes indicate that members also volunteered time for projects for both the Red Cross and the Salvation Army. Care packages for the congregation's service members stationed overseas contained nonperishables and news from home to help lift spirits and quell homesickness.

With most able-bodied men fighting the war, labor shortages during harvesting season became problematic. To help alleviate the shortages, farmers were able to enlist the help of POWs. County extension agents, such as William Tolley, helped coordinate the needs of farmers throughout the area with Camp Forrest commanders. He would sometimes drive to Camp Forrest to pick up guards and POWs and drop them off at farms throughout Moore County. His daughter, Nina, would occasionally ride with him on his trips to Camp Forrest. She recalled one trip when the bushes along the road rose up and began walking around. She gasped and then realized it was only soldiers on maneuvers.[166] Farmers with especially large farms were happy to have the extra help during harvest season. McKelvey[167] had a 140-acre farm and employed dozens of POWs to help. He found that the men were respectful and hardworking and did not have or seem to require any guards to oversee them.

Love, Marriage and Baby Carriages

Before the war, there were socially established conventions that young people followed, from meeting to dating, which could culminate in going steady and eventually getting married. Perhaps errors in judgements were normal under the suspension of traditional conventions due to war. Juvenile promiscuity, professional prostitution and venereal disease became ever-increasing social issues during the war. However, in general, love and marriage was always in bloom in Tullahoma. Often, girlfriends became wives after traveling from long distances to Tullahoma by themselves. Families such as the Couches helped many a young bride obtain her wedding trousseau during the hustle and bustle of war preparations. Searcy Hopkins and Dot Couch Watson remember fondly how their mother, Anabel, helped one young bride find a pair of wedding shoes. It was no small task, since shoes were on the list of rationed goods and her feet were larger than normal. Anabel located a pair of white satin house slippers that completed the ensemble. At another wedding, Searcy Hopkins served as maid of honor for Mary Louise Morris, who had arrived in town shortly before her betrothed, Corporal Ivan E.

Miller, shipped out. Since she did not know anyone in town, she asked Searcy to participate in the wedding. People were so happy to be with their loved ones that "culture clashes" were generally nonexistent. There were numerous instances of couples meeting and falling in love at Camp Forrest, including Chuck and Hannah Tyler. He was a soldier of the Thirty-Third Division from Chicago, and she was a civilian from the area in charge of personnel. Chuck eventually transferred to the Post Engineers, given his expertise in plumbing. They married in late 1943 before he left for Europe and were married for sixty-eight years.

With Camp Forrest being its own "town," it was listed as the place of birth on the birth certificates of babies born at the Station Hospital. The first baby born at Camp Forrest was Stanley Richard Taylor, son of Private Stanley and Flossie Nell Taylor of Illinois, born on July 4, 1941. Robby Armstrong's[168] father, Staff Sergeant Robert Armstrong, was the head baker at the Camp Forrest Cooks and Bakers School. His mother stayed in town but delivered her newborn on base. Judy Turchin[169] was a toddler when her mother was pregnant with her sister. Her mother was set to deliver in Nashville, but she went into labor early. The family rushed her to the Station Hospital at Camp Forrest. Luckily, one of the German POWs was a leading OBGYN in Germany. Mother and baby came through the delivery process in good health. Within hours, the premature baby was transported to Nashville. She stayed at the Nashville hospital for several months until she had gained enough weight to come home. According to the Social Security Administration, the top baby names in the 1940s for boys were James, Robert and John. Top names for girls included Mary, Linda and Barbara.

ENEMY, FRENEMY AND FRIEND

GERMAN PRISONERS OF WAR

W hen the United States became a participant in World War II, Great Britain requested assistance in helping reduce its overcrowded prisoner of war (POW) population. Although woefully ill prepared and inexperienced in detaining international POWs, the U.S. federal government agreed to assist. Each month soon thereafter, approximately thirty thousand Axis combatants captured by Allied forces arrived on American soil via returning troop ships.

ADMINISTRATION OF U.S. PRISONER OF WAR SYSTEM

The Office of the Provost Marshal General was responsible for the housing and day-to-day care of captives held throughout the United States. The provisions outlined in the Geneva Convention (1929) detailed the administration of all POW-related activities. From this treaty, participating nations adopted the position that at a minimum the care of captives mirrored the care a nation supplied its own service members. Unlike many nations, the United States elected to enforce the provisions to the letter of the law. The International Red Cross, the International YMCA, Swiss diplomats and U.S. government officials enforced the Convention's standards via periodic visits to each facility. Officials held steadfast in this decision in the hopes that other warring nations would follow suit in the treatment of the captives they held, especially American service members.[170] Although the federal government was merely following treaties established before its entry into the war, U.S. citizens found some of the prisoner accommodations more akin to hosting a friend rather than detaining an enemy.

Amid language barriers and the existence of very few armed guards or security at the encampments, each POW facility reported little disruption and few escape attempts given the overall large captive populations. Unlike Great Britain, the United States typically allowed prisoners to establish their own hierarchy and to manage themselves. The federal government attempted to conceal the nationality of internees from the public for fear of reprisal and hysteria. However, neighboring communities were generally fully aware of their identity. In many towns, names such as "JAP camp" or "Fritz Ritz" were the predominant references to the camps. These derogatory names did not necessarily reflect the cultural background of the detainees. Although there were over 425,000 prisoners throughout the United States, there are no widespread reports of citizen hostilities directed toward POWs or the encampments in the five years the POW program was active.

In general, these enemies of the state soon developed lifelong friendships with their captors and won over many townspeople. The narratives of Middle Tennesseans and/or their descendants regarding POW interactions, the narratives from POW letters sent to friends and family in Germany and artwork samples created by POWs underscore how many of the individuals from this era transformed their perceptions of the most hated World War II enemies into friendships.

The Enemy

Geneva Convention provisions stipulated that housing and food for POWs be in the same manner as the belligerent's servicemen. Citizens were outraged not only due to the perceived higher level of "care" being administered, but also that POWs could readily obtain many rationed products. These items were readily and continually available throughout the war to POWs at PXs or at meals. The federal government believed adhering strictly to the terms of the Geneva Convention would convince Axis nations to provide a similar level of treatment to American prisoners of war. Unfortunately, U.S. soldiers endured harsh living conditions and deprivation of food and water for extended periods.

Newspaper accounts in the *Jackson Sun*[171] reported allegations that prisoners received disproportionate amounts of meat in comparison to civilians. Before a full congressional investigation convened, the complainant dropped the charges based on misinformation. The *Sheboygan Press*[172] reported that breakfast for prisoners consisted of milk, soup, coffee cake, coffee and bread; lunch consisted of a bean soup, bread and tea; and dinners consisted of fricassee, boiled potatoes, coleslaw, bread and coffee. Eventually, base commanders allowed POWs to prepare Germanic-based meals, which helped decrease food waste considerably. One such Germanic preference was dark breads rather than the traditional American white bread. In March 1945, the *Tennessean*[173] reported that German POW cooks eliminated fresh meats in favor of salt pork, bologna, salami, frankfurters and cheese.

Many German POW interviews and articles noted how men were ready to surrender to American or British troops as soon as possible. Each soldier was aware of how Axis and Allied powers treated captives. These men did not willingly volunteer for Hitler's armies and now wished to return home to family and friends once the war ended. Then, as today, the vivid images of death and destruction caused by the German army throughout Europe are horrific. However, scholars such as Arnold Kramer in *Nazi Prisoners of War in America* suggest that only a small portion of the overall German POW population held in the United States were extreme enemy combatants, such as SS and Wehrmacht soldiers. The hundreds of thousands of remaining German captives generally coexisted peacefully and happily in the various camps. From these accounts, it would seem the small number of hardened SS and Wehrmacht soldiers were mainly guilty of continually attempting to cause strife at POW facilities. Punishments for disruptive or unruly prisoners included cutting off hot-water supplies or closing the PX. As compensation, prisoners received canteen coupons, so being unable to purchase supplies of American goods at the PX was intolerable.

From Propaganda to Detainment Processing

Propaganda in the United States portrayed Germans as cruel and evil beings intent on overtaking the world. Equally, Hitler and Joseph Goebbels were adept at using propaganda to persuade compatriots into a specific mentality that supported the war and acts of inhumanity. Posters were effective tools used by both sides to spur citizens to give more for the war effort. Their usage

American propaganda poster produced by the Office of War Information. Posters promoted particular behaviors the government felt would help win the war. *NARA-CP*.

German propaganda featuring Roosevelt, Churchill and Stalin, alleging that these leaders started the war with the backing of the Jews. *National Holocaust Museum.*

of propaganda took stereotypes and discrimination of certain populations to a new level. Some individuals bought into these messages wholeheartedly, while others were not as ardent supporters.

From approximately 1942 to 1946, more than 425,000 prisoners of war arrived in the United States on returning Liberty ships. After arrival at one of the Eastern Seaboard ports of debarkation, men were processed and assigned to one of seven hundred POW camps in the United States. Of the eleven facilities located in Tennessee, four were main camps and seven had branch camp classification. The construction of main camps, such as Camp Forrest, was done according to military specifications, whereas branch camps utilized current structures within the community, such as school buildings, fairgrounds or old Civilian Conservation Corps (CCC) camps. Two of the largest main camp facilities were located in Middle Tennessee: Camp Forrest and Camp Crossville. Each facility primarily housed German captives (approximately 3,000 and 1,500, respectively), but small populations of Italian and Japanese captives were detained at each one. According to the *Jackson Sun*, the War Department reclassified Camp Forrest from a military training and induction facility to a prisoner of war general hospital and camp in spring 1944.[174] Camp Crossville was reportedly an officer's camp, although its administration was similar to other noncommissioned officer POW camps. Some officer-designated camps had individual bungalows as living quarters for each officer instead of shared huts.[175]

Although unspeakable acts occurred in Germany, curious townspeople, both young and old, congregated around incoming trains to see exactly how an enemy looked. Many descendants of Tullahoma residents recounted family lore of relatives looking in earnest for a prisoner's "tail and horns." Individuals have yet to end a story by saying that the family member saw those devilish appendages! Appearances of German soldiers varied, from blond hair and blue eyes to dark hair and brown eyes; the only general differentiating quality was the German language spoken. However, some were fluent in English and could easily blend in with citizens. In fact, several escapees were able to blend into their environments and remain undetected before recapture. Bob Couch often recounted the story of a Tullahoma resident mistaking a POW for a guard, as the man spoke fluent English, even with a hint of a southern accent. Once the prisoner corrected her on his nationality, she asked how he learned to speak English so well. He indicated that although he was of German descent, he had been raised in East Tennessee. War broke out during his visit to relatives in Germany. Unfortunately, he was unable to leave the country at that point and eventually was conscripted into the Nazi army. Perceptions of both citizen and combatant began to transition from enemy to frenemy.

THE FRENEMY

A frenemy is an individual who pretends to be a friend but in actuality is an enemy or has an underlying motive. The shift in the perceptions from enemy to frenemy among guards and prisoners may have occurred due to understaffing issues at camps, as well as the general adherence and compliance to the rules and regulations by significant portions of prisoners. The apprehension felt by both parties gave way to a mutual understanding and respect for one another, and over time bonds and personal relationships evolved. Undersupplied security forces typically consisted of soldiers deemed unfit for combat based on medical and psychological reasons.

Many Camp Forrest POWs worked to pass the time and eliminate boredom. Under the Geneva Convention, work could be required of noncommissioned soldiers, but it was optional for officers. Any form of work was acceptable as long as it did not directly support the war effort or was dangerous to the health and well-being of the prisoner. Given the shortage of labor due to the war, POWs contributed greatly to the nation's economy. Reports from the Provost General Marshal's Office indicate the nation reaped over $34 billion in man-day labor.[176] During harvesting, farmers were able to secure much-needed help from POWs so that crops would not wither. There were many instances of POWs being transferred to camps in other states during peak harvesting times. Many news reports noted that a returning soldier or citizen could obtain a job currently filled by a POW; no one would be unemployed due to POWs.

Noncommissioned POWs received $0.80 per day (approximately $11.60 in 2018) of working, based on the prevailing rates for the nation's enlisted personnel. Of the $1.50 (approximately $22.00 in 2018) collected from those employing POWs, $0.80 went to the POW, while the federal government used the balance to defray food and housing costs. The *Kingsport News*[177] reported that for civilian labor the army would have incurred an additional cost of $3.52 per man per day for the completion of similar tasks. POWs could obtain pay via coupons to purchase items in the camp's canteen. It was also possible to save one's monies until it was time to leave for home. Detailed records maintained by individual camps and the Provost Marshal General's Office helped ensure that each prisoner received all of his remaining earnings on repatriation. Fraternizing with POWs was a serious infraction; women who did socialize with them faced dismissal from their job and were escorted off the base. POWs faced transfers to another camp for such infractions.

Prisoner escapes occurred, but instances of public mass hysteria and sabotage feared by the federal government never occurred. The *St. Louis Star and Times*[178] reported in February 1948 that 2,803 prisoners of war escaped during the war years. It further noted that only 18 were still at large. The FBI asked citizens to report anyone matching the alleged escapees' descriptions. When residents learned of someone escaping, everyone retreated inside, locking doors and windows. Once news of the individual's recapture reached residents, normal daily activities resumed. Many of the escapees returned to the camp after either a few hours or days on the run. Staying on the run required more effort than most prisoners were willing to expend. Once this information was reported, anxiety over the frenemy's covert intentions for escape diminished.

Even in death, POWs received the same level of dignity and respect extended to American service members. Government records indicate that approximately eighty-seven POWs died at Camp Forrest: seventy-four from natural causes, four killed in accidents, one died while escaping, one killed attacking a guard and seven from suicide. The Tullahoma funeral home Daves Culbertson Funeral Home prepared bodies for burial per government contract stipulations. While seventy-three POWs reportedly died of natural causes, memories of the guards and others working at Camp Forrest reveal that there were far more suicides than officially reported. Generally, misidentifying the cause of death occurred to avoid potential

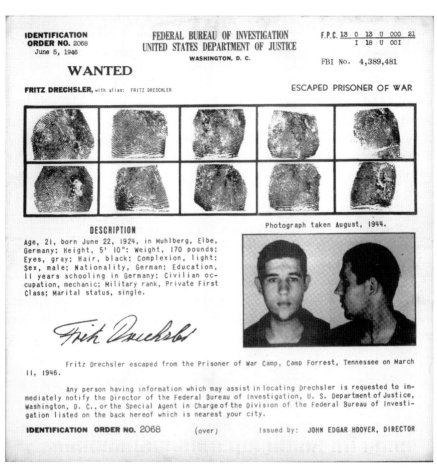

FBI wanted poster for POW escapee Fritz Drechsler. He evaded capture until becoming overwhelmed with hunger and seeking shelter in a barn. *Author's collection.*

government investigations and civilian rumors. Several employees at Camp Forrest remember German POWs shot during escape attempts. Eva Jean Hildman[179] was having lunch outside the laundry facility one afternoon when piercing gunshots rang out. Many of the women enjoying lunch outside that afternoon assumed the shots were from the firing range. However, it was later rumored that the shots were fired during an escape attempt that resulted in a POW dying.

In 1943, Curtis Cobb[180] worked at Ramsey Funeral Home on South Jackson Street. One spring morning, the funeral home director asked him to drive the hearse for the graveside service of a POW. The detainee had died from twenty-seven gunshot wounds fired from a guard's machine gun during an escape attempt. Onlookers were unaware of the decedent's nationality as the hearse made its way to the pauper section of Maplewood Cemetery. Shortly after Cobb's arrival at the gravesite, four jeeps with two machine guns mounted on the front of their hood and four large army transport trucks pulled up. A guard gave a signal, and approximately thirty-six men per truck disembarked and lined up around the casket. Cobb remembered the wreath that several POWs laid on the casket. Not having the funds to purchase one from a flower shop, the men made one from wire coat hangers, oak leaves and wildflowers. It was just as lovely as one prepared by a florist. The officiants for the service were both an American and a German chaplain. Once the service was over, the POWs returned to the trucks for the drive back to base. Other reports indicate that some funerals included full German military services, replete with a Nazi Germany state flag (*swastika*) draped over the coffin. Soldiers were restricted to wearing clothes with large stenciled *PW* on them, except during funerals. The prisoners could wear their military dress uniforms when attending a funeral. Many towns protested having prisoners interred in local cemeteries. Burials occurred on base grounds until the authorities could reinter them at a military cemetery, such as the Chattanooga National Cemetery.

The Friend

Friendships emerge from the most unlikely of places and circumstances. Many prisoners were excited to go to work each day—not just to relieve boredom or earn money, but to connect with new friends and enjoy home-cooked meals. Many prisoners became so trusted that they left the encampment for work in the morning and returned in the evening without a guard or any other supervision. Prisoners' verbal promises not to escape evolved into a bond of trust between captive and captor. For many of these individuals, it was unnecessary to share a language in order to share a friendship. However, many Germans believed that their homeland would win the war and often explained this fact to their captors. While they did not believe in the Nazi rhetoric, the war reports they read and heard of Germany's destruction were only propaganda to them.

Individuals throughout camps were from varied ideological backgrounds, ranging from ardent Nazi supporters to anti-Nazis. Noted historian Dr. Michael Bradley reported that eight different European languages were spoken throughout the facility.[181] Camp Forrest's commanding officers maintained detailed records of name, rank, ideology and behavior of POWs and sent regular reports to the Office of the Provost Marshal General in Washington. It was extremely important to monitor the activities of suspected ardent Nazi supporters, as they tended to view anti-Nazis as traitors. The nonsupporters were either terrorized or killed via organized attacks in an effort to exact punishment. Declassified records obtained from the National Archives and Records Administration detail numerous letters from non-Nazi supporters sent to the commanding officer of the prisoner of war camp indicating death threats based on nationality. Many individuals fortunately received protective custody and eventually were transferred to another POW facility. Others were not as fortunate, as Nazi justice was typically swift and silent. Victims of the vigilante justice were found dead of apparent suicides the next morning. Death reports do not reflect high numbers of homicides, as these deaths were ruled suicides. Individuals who knew the truth were reluctant to report the facts, fearing the same end might befall them.

POW leisure time was full of activities, such as taking education courses, playing and listening to music, producing plays, producing newsletters, playing sports and drawing, painting and sculpting. The Germans who participated in the orchestra typically had professional musical backgrounds and played a variety of instruments, including violin, trumpet, piano, cello and saxophone. Throughout the encampment, there were approximately sixty-three different classes taught by forty teachers. Forty men sang various classical and modern German and American songs in the choir.

In addition to private purchases by the base, the War Prisoner Aid division of the YMCA and International Red Cross donated books for the base library. The POW library was located in the Red Cross building of General Hospital No. 2. Reports indicate that almost half of the four thousand books were in need of repair; the remaining 50 percent were constantly in circulation. Almost 80 percent of the POWs used the library and reading room facilities. Accessible current newspapers and magazines included the *New York Times*, *Nashville Banner*, *Readers Digest*, *Look*, *Life*, *Time*, *Fortune* and *Nashville Tennessean*. Articles censored by base commanders were cut out of the various newspapers and magazines before being distributed to POWs. There was considerable need for textbooks, as there were courses on history, English, biology, languages, shorthand, mathematics and geography. Favorite outdoor recreational activities included track and soccer, and indoor recreational activities included chess, checkers, Ping-Pong and cards. Prisoners engaged in a number of hobbies, including

Camp Forrest German POW orchestra. Camp employees recall the beautiful sounds of music filtering through the camp as the band practiced. *Author's collection.*

painting, wood carving, acting, singing and playing musical instruments. Ample radios were available throughout the camp, broadcasting a variety of programs. The church doubled as a movie theater and had seating capacity for 250 individuals. Guarded POWs were also allowed to go to the movie theaters in Tullahoma.

Labor reports issued by Camp Forrest indicate that POWs worked in divisions, such as the bakery, laundry, grounds and roads, mess hall, vehicle maintenance, canteen and hospital. In addition, there were private agriculture contract workers. Given the shortages of labor due to able-bodied men fighting overseas or working in armed forces–related industries, it was critical to have POW labor to ensure crops did not wither in the fields. Government field reports indicated that Camp Forrest had three branch camps: Tellico Plains, Huntsville Arsenal and Lawrenceburg. Although only a few translators were located at each camp, men not only overcame language barriers by learning and improving English-language skills but also used nonverbal cues and had a mutual respect for one another. Individuals who visited or worked at Camp Forrest or those who recollected stories from relatives reflected on numerous companionable encounters with POWs.

At age fifteen, Watson Hensley[182] began delivering milk for Columbia Dairy to Camp Forrest and befriended a young German prisoner who was always eager to help him unload the milk. In appreciation for his help, Hensley gave the POW a pint-sized bottle of chocolate milk each visit. The German had never had chocolate milk but found it delicious after just a few sips. In addition to delivering milk, Hensley was responsible for picking up empty bottles at the base. The POWs would load and unload the dairy's bottles. He was still able to communicate well with these men amid the language barriers. One of the POWs he saw regularly offered his daughter's hand in marriage! These men shared appreciation and camaraderie for one another over simple acts of kindness—not enemies, but friends.[183]

German medical officers and technicians were under the supervision of a small staff of American medical officers at the Station Hospital. These international practitioners treated both prisoners and American GIs. Civilians still worked throughout the Station Hospital after it transitioned to a POW facility. Margaret Templeton Tolley[184] graduated from Nashville Business School and obtained an administrative assistant position at the Station Hospital. She worked for several high-level hospital administrators, including Colonel Hannah. She had a wonderful working relationship with Colonel Hannah, who told her he would readily rehire her whether at Camp Forrest or in a civilian setting. His wife, Ann, would send her delightful care packages of cakes and candies. While language barriers typically prevented conversations between the non-English-speaking Germans and Americans, Margaret said the individuals she encountered were always pleasant and respectful. No POW incidents or problems were reported during her time at the hospital. The prisoners created numerous beautiful gardens throughout the hospital grounds. A POW created five watercolor paintings of nature scenes for her that have become family heirlooms.

Government reports indicate that a visit from YMCA delegates and representative Edouard Patte commended Camp Forrest on the physical and psychological well-being of POWs convalescing in the facility. He denoted that the comedy play and symphony concert put on by POWs were extremely entertaining. Patte further reported the existence of an impressive number of programs, such as education courses, orchestra and sporting activities that POWs could participate in. After the visit, the delegates decided the YMCA would supply more sporting equipment rather than musical instruments in the coming months for the detainees. He was impressed by how well the large facility was maintained, specifically noting the landscaping, paved roads and building maintenance by civilian personnel aided by German POWs. The tour also included visits with German chaplains and pastors and an inspection of the chapel. The chapel had pews where groups could congregate for services, Bible study and choir practice.

Huntsville, Alabama's Red Stone Arsenal was a POW branch camp. In spring 1943, Al Bradley[185] was an electrician building POW barracks at Red Stone. Initially, the only electricity in each barrack was a single light bulb hanging from the center of the room. Several months after initial construction, electricians installed wall outlets. He recalled that many of the Germans spoke fluent English, as he had spent time talking with many of them.

On May 7, 1945, Germany unconditionally surrendered to Allied forces in Reims, France. The surrender took effect the next day with a declaration of Victory in Europe (VE) Day. Back on the home front, most of the guards who worked at Red Stone were enjoying a movie. After stopping the movie, an announcement was made that all patrons who were guards needed to report to the base immediately. Officials feared POWs would riot when they learned of Germany's surrender. Base commander Captain Johnson made the announcement after calling all POWs to the center of the camp. When his commanding voice boomed across the crowd, he said there would be no rioting and that everyone was to return to his tent and under no circumstances leave it until morning. There were no incidents that night there or at Camp Forrest as a result of Germany's surrender.

Bradley recalled a humorous incident he witnessed one afternoon between two POWs. Transfers in and out of the facility were routine. He observed that two POWs met and hugged each other; one man was in a German military uniform, and the other was in POW garments. The apparent joyous reunion turned hostile as each man began hollering at the other. After parting ways, Bradley asked the man clad in POW garb what occurred. The POW proceeded to tell him that the man in the uniform was his cousin, whom he had not seen since the war broke out. His cousin claimed that he did not join the German army voluntarily. The man replied that he understood, as his service was also forced. However, he replied to his cousin that the Wehrmacht did not force him to get those corporal stripes.

The POW letters sent home were subjected to review by both American and German censors. The censors were looking for subversive materials embedded in the stationery paper or codes within the text. Of the letters examined thus far by researchers, POWs often penned how they longed to be home with loved ones. In his letter to his wife, Heini Ackermann was delighted to learn that his wife in Germany had become friends with the wife of one of his fellow Camp Forrest detainees. Both men were glad the women had befriended each other.

Once repatriated, the POWs continued their letter writing, but now it was to the men and women who had befriended them during their time in Tennessee. Each letter details fond memories and events that took place in their lives as they and their country worked to overcome the devastation and destruction of the war. It was a time of war, but amid the hostilities, many Tennesseans chose humanity and compassion toward an "enemy of the state."

Repatriation started in 1944, but the process was slow, as the need for labor for harvesting and various industries was still high. Federal government

Above and opposite: Two of five watercolor paintings of outdoor scenes created by a Camp Forrest POW as a gift for Margaret Templeton Tolley, who worked at the camp's hospital. She was the administrative assistant to Colonel Hannah until the end of the war. *Lynn Tolley family collection*.

MESSAGE
All communications should be of strictly private nature only.
Please write very clearly and on the lines.
NACHRICHT
Ausschliesslich Familiennachrichten.
Bitte deutlich und auf der Linie schreiben.
MESSAGGIO
Ogni communicazione dev'essere soltanto di carattere strettamente personale.
Si prega di scrivere chiaramente sulle linee.

CENSORSHIP ★ EXAMINED By 503

Meine Lieben. Falls Ihr noch keine Nachricht
habt, bin in amerikanischer Gefangenschaft.
Bin gesund und hoffe dasselbe von Euch.
Bitte gleich Rückantwort.
                    Gruss Euer Papa

Date / Datum / Data **12. 8. 43**
Signature / Unterschrift / Firma **Erwin Neubauer**

Postage free unless sent by Air Mail.
Portofrei—Bei Luftpostbeförderung muss die Luftpostgebühr bezahlt werden.
Spedizione gratis a meno che sia fatta per posta aerea.

Left: German POW letter sent to family back home delivered by the Red Cross. The prisoners could write or receive a message via the Red Cross. *Author's collection.*

Below: German POWs wrote letters home wanting to hear if loved ones and friends were doing well. Many letters remarked that the individual was well treated. *Author's collection.*

U.S.A., DEN 18. MAERZ 1946
LIEBE ELTERN! AM 15. MAERZ 46 EUREN BRIEF VOM
2.1.46 MIT GROSSER FREUDE ERHALTEN. WIE IHR
SCHREIBT IST ZUHAUSE ALLES GESUND, DASS IST
DIE HAUPTSACHE LIEBE ELTERN ICH BIN SOMIT
EINER GROSSEN SORGE ENTLASTET. UM MICH
BRAUCHT IHR EUCH NICHT ZU SORGEN, BIN
GESUND. UEBERMITTLE EUCH DIE HERZLICHSTEN
GRUESSE UND BESTEN WUENSCHE! Adolf

pressure to process out all POWs sped up the repatriation process, and the last POW left Camp Forrest on April 13, 1946. Once the war was over, the Geneva Convention provisions were relaxed, and the three delicious meals a day became peanut butter sandwiches. Before being repatriated, all POWS were forced to view films depicting the horrors of the Nazi concentration camps. Some of the men believed the films were American propaganda; others were horrified at the acts of their countrymen.

Once repatriated, POWs returned to a country ravaged by both a war and a maniacal dictator. Many of the former Camp Forrest POWs were able to locate families and friends and start the arduous journey of rebuilding their lives and their country. Although there was very little clothing and food available on their return, many men found the time and resources to write to those who had befriended them during their time at Camp Forrest. Letters detailed daily life and dreams for the future. Some continued to send artwork and homeland items, such as tablecloths, to their American friends. In a touching letter, Alfred Arbatzat wrote to William Brasher, who was in the engineering division when he met the POW. Arbatzat was a groundskeeper under Brasher. He described how much he appreciated his decent treatment and that he enjoyed working for him. He wrote that he was able to find work on a farm on his return to Germany. Arbatzat wanted to maintain contact with the Brasher family and provided an address so he could correspond. These stories underscore the importance of not placing individuals into stereotypes or cultural generalizations. An enemy might actually become a friend at the end of the day.

AFTERMATH OF WAR

When Camp Forrest and Northern Field were decommissioned, the population and influx of monies to Tullahoma and the surrounding counties plummeted. The encampment was only six years old when the war ended, and the government declared it surplus. Throughout the Southeast, items from barracks and chapels to recreation and office equipment found new use in civilian and commercial settings. Congregations such as Hope Baptist Church and Mimosa Church of Christ of Lincoln County used base chapels, which provided communities with new religious facilities.[186] In a feature on the Mimosa Church of Christ, the *Tullahoma News* indicated that the congregation purchased its chapel in 1946 for $900 ($10,650 in 2018). The price was a bargain, as the original cost to construct each one of the nine chapels, complete with stained woodwork, on Camp Forrest was $21,000 ($248,488 in 2018). Although renovations have occurred over the years, some of the adornments, such as light fixtures and altar rails, from the original chapels still exist.[187] Henry C. Beck Contracting dismantled and packaged many of the buildings destined for colleges so that the institutions could easily reassemble them.[188] The Federal Public Housing Authority awarded the company the contract to complete the work. From induction and training of over 250,000 soldiers, to employing more than 12,000 civilians and housing 22,000 prisoners of war, Camp Forrest had done its part of help win the Second World War. Over 28,000 construction workers were responsible for helping transform the state

The chapel of the 129th Infantry Regiment on Easter morning 1942. Field services were held on the regimental parade ground earlier that morning. *NARA-CP*.

guard facility Camp Peay into the city-sized army installation. Uncle Sam's nieces and nephews in Tullahoma did their part to help ensure the war ended quickly and that as many soldiers as possible returned home safely.

IMPACT OF DECOMMISSIONING
AND NATIONAL PRIORITIES

Reports in early 1944 indicated that Camp Forrest would continue to operate after the war. The jubilation of VE-Day quickly shifted to one of concern regarding the fate of Camp Forrest. By March 1946, Tennessee senator Tom Stewart urged Assistant Secretary of War Stimson to keep the base open due to current world events. He noted in his correspondence, "the war department had a great opportunity to take over an already-established and thoroughly well rounded camp site with everything from horses to heavy artillery."[189] Unfortunately, his efforts were in vain, as the War Department proceeded with the decommissioning process. Under the lease agreement with the state, the federal government was obligated to return the surrounding lands to their original condition. However, the governor, other local city officials and businessmen requested that amenities, such as the roads and railroads remain intact rather than be destroyed. The city purchased numerous federal government structures at a fraction of the original construction costs. Some of the buildings included Tullahoma Community Center, Red Cross Chapter house, water filtration and sewage disposal systems and the East Lincoln Street Grammar School. The Camp Forrest USO building became a community center in town, but fire destroyed the structure in February 1949.[190]

The facility was deactivated as an army post on May 31, 1946. However, there was still much activity at Camp Forrest, as POWs were not yet repatriated. In town, the once overcrowded sidewalks and the constantly gridlocked streets started to clear, enabling residents to visit town more regularly. Eventually, dismantled barracks found new lives as homes, barns and schools throughout the state. The October 31, 1946[191] edition of the *Tennessean* reported that Peabody College submitted an application to the Federal Works Authority in Atlanta for ten classroom buildings, an assembly room and a cafeteria with its equipment. The Federal Works Authority sold several buildings to North Georgia College in Dahlonega, Georgia. Educational institutions had first priority to obtain buildings and other surplus items from inactivated military installations, as the federal government anticipated an influx of returning veterans on college campuses. These individuals could take advantage of the newly instituted GI Bill. Ads and editorials regarding the surplus sales at Camp Forrest appeared throughout the Southeast. Religious organizations obtained several chapels. Many of these buildings are still located in communities throughout Middle

Tennessee. The Camp Forrest sports arena was re-christened the Mary Mars Gymnasium at Lincoln Memorial University in Harrogate, Tennessee.

Eventually, Tennessee state officials decided to deed the Camp Forrest environs and thousands of additional acreage to the federal government in a deal to transform the site into the nation's first major U.S. Air Force testing facility for aircraft and wind tunnels, Arnold Engineering Development Center (AEDC). The proposed site encompassed approximately forty thousand acres. President Truman presided over the dedication of the facility on June 25, 1951. The dedication and naming honored five-star general of the U.S. Air Force Henry "Hap" Arnold, the "father" of the modern air force. Although he had passed away the preceding January, his wife, Eleanor, and sons, David, William and Henry, were at the dedication ceremony. President Truman arrived that warm Monday morning via the plane *Independence* at Northern Field to a crowd of anxious Tennesseans. He rode through Tullahoma in an open-top convertible, which the Duckworth family loaned for the event. Cheering crowds packed both sides of the streets along the parade route.[192] The ceremony took place at the proposed AEDC site, and an air show entertained the crowd with flyovers from numerous flying machines from bygone eras to the present. The Maxwell House from Nashville catered a fried chicken and apple pie luncheon afterward.

No details were left to chance for this official occasion. The dedication committee built a briefing area and green room to give the president and his platform party time to relax and prepare for the festivities. Tullahoma's Rollins & Levan Furniture Store beautifully appointed the entire green room. Former Camp Forrest base commander Major General Franklin Carroll sent a letter of thanks to A.J. Rollins for his and Hawkersmith's generosity in preparing the room at no expense to the federal government. Hawkersmith's daughter, Joanne, who was a toddler at the time, vividly remembers that the room contained not only chairs and tables but also lamps and pictures on the wall. After the ceremony, the store sold the furnishings, but the chair Truman sat in became part of the AEDC archives collection. Although the president's time in this once bustling military town was only a short five hours, the event gave Tullahomans renewed hope that their current economic downturn would soon reverse itself.

Local weather conditions and the Korean War delayed the groundbreaking construction on the facility. According to the inserts on the golden anniversary of Arnold Engineering Development Center[193] in the *Tullahoma News*, conflicting federal priorities due to the Korean War persisted for three years. However, military and political leaders remained

Above: The presidential motorcade leaving William Northern Field and driving through Tullahoma to the future site of Arnold Engineering Development Center for its June 25, 1951 dedication ceremony. *NARA-CP*.

Right: President Truman prepares his dedication ceremony speech. In the background is a photo of Henry Harley "Hap" Arnold, founding father of the U.S. Air Force. *NARA-CP*.

steadfast in their conviction that the facility was essential for ensuring that the United States remained ahead of other nations in this arena. It took approximately six years to finish the facility. As each of the four complexes was completed, testing commenced. It took approximately six years at a cost of $150,000,000 (approximately $4,930,480,000 in 2018) to complete. Numerous construction workers and military and civilian employees settled in Tullahoma because of AEDC. The influx of people and monies never revived the World War II era. In fiscal year 2000, the total economic impact of AEDC was $499.1 million, and the employment impact in Tennessee was approximately three thousand jobs.

LOCAL PERSPECTIVES ON THE AFTERMATH OF WAR

Individuals still vividly remember Camp Forrest's dismantling and the surplus sale days after the mighty cantonment was decommissioned. Although the area had numerous pre- and postwar industries, such as the General Shoe Company, Worth Sporting Equipment and Bulls Eye Overalls, these industries in postwar times experienced an economic downturn as government demand for mass quantities of supplies ceased. For example, in the war years, the General Shoe Company altered its manufacturing to produce army boots and repair military personnel shoes. Robert Spinney[194] reported that General Shoe received a total of over $4.6 million in defense contracts (approximately $73.8 million in 2018) from 1941 to 1945.

Even organizations such as churches felt the economic downturn. The First Baptist Church of Tullahoma planned to construct a new education building due to the economic boom. However, the construction plans for an auditorium took longer than anticipated, and funds were no longer as readily available. The church experienced continual growth in the ensuing decades, which allowed it to develop and expand activities and missionary work.

Bob Couch[195] retrieved and cared for the American flag that had flown so proudly in front of the headquarters building. He offered veterans who returned to Tullahoma a small swatch of that flag as a remembrance of the time spent at Camp Forrest and as a thank-you for their service. The flag is now on display at the Sam H. Werner Military Museum in Monteagle, Tennessee. Bob also ran the local photography store during World War II and developed the film rolls that soldiers brought in. He remembered some

Camp Forrest Headquarters on June 24, 1942. Tullahoma native Robert "Bob" Couch lowered the flag for the last time in late 1946. *NARA-CP.*

soldiers shipped out before they could pick up their film. He tried for years to locate the soldiers in an effort to return the photos. Unfortunately, many envelopes were returned marked "killed in action." So many of our warriors never knew the victories of the war, as death came all too soon.

In 1986, Governor Lamar Alexander initiated a statewide homecoming celebration. For its part in the festivities, Tullahoma held a Camp Forrest reunion. The reunion was an opportunity for visitors and veterans and their survivors to visit the area and participate in a USO dance, a parade and the dedication of a monument at the old main gate area for the encampment. The impressive granite monument lists the units known to have trained at Camp Forrest.[196] Many of the German prisoners of war returned for the event. Camp Forrest will always endure as a vital part of history.

NOTES

Introduction

1. Justice, "Camp Forrest Research."
2. "National Guard's Camp Peay Became Army's Camp Forrest."
3. Yarbrough, "Italians and Germans Have Easy Life."

Chapter 1

4. Searcy Couch Hopkins and Dorothy Couch Watson, transcript of oral history, conducted 2013, MT2013.512, Albert Gore Research Center, Middle Tennessee State University, Murfreesboro, Tennessee
5. James O. Gist Sr., transcript of oral history conducted in 2000, MT2000.026, Albert Gore Research Center.
6. Robert L. "Bob" Couch Jr., transcript of oral history conducted in 2001, MT2001.035, Albert Gore Research Center.
7. Von Messling, "Cousins Remember Tullahoman Shares."
8. Mosely, "Tullahoma Was Already in a Military State."
9. Paris Brewer, transcript of oral history conducted in 2002, MT2002.98, Albert Gore Research Center.
10. Dlorice Stanaland, transcript of oral history conducted in 2008 by Jacob Worthington for World History Major Semester Project.

11. Alan Gray, unpublished face-to-face interview by Dr. Elizabeth Taylor, conducted October 17, 2018.
12. "General Ben Lear Sounds Warning."
13. Harry Pavey, transcript of oral history conducted in 1993, T-63, in Tullahoma, Tennessee, audiocassette, Motlow State Community College, Tullahoma, Tennessee.
14. Allen Wesley Kirby Collection (AFC/2001/001/69033), Veterans History Project, American Folklife Center, Library of Congress.
15. Richard Albert Koepke Collection (AFC/2001/001/82134), Veterans History Project.
16. "Yule Spirit to Be Present in Camp Forrest," *Decatur Daily Review*, December 22, 1941.

Chapter 2

17. "'Speculation' Camp Threat, Says Frazier," *Tennessean*.
18. Bradley, "Reveille to Taps."
19. "War Department Lets Construction Contracts."
20. Lee Beavers, transcript of oral history conducted in 1993, E-23, in Tullahoma, Tennessee, audiocassette, Motlow State Community College.
21. James Spence, transcript of oral history conducted in 1993, C-20, in Normandy, Tennessee, audiocassette, Motlow State Community College.
22. Powell, "Boom-Dazed Tullahoma Awakes."
23. "CCC at Camp Forrest," *Daily Times*, May 24, 1941.
24. Northcutt, "Blacks an Integral Part."
25. "Wage Rate Set at Camp Peay."
26. "Camp Forrest Ready for Soldiers from Four States."
27. "Camp Peay Has Lumber Shortages."
28. Gowran, "Illinois Troops Will Find Camp Morass of Mud."
29. "Camp Forrest," *Austin American*.
30. Dudley Tipps, unpublished interview with Dr. Elizabeth Taylor, South Jackson Civic Center, October 17, 2018.
31. "Gen. Forrest Honored by War Body in Renaming Camp Peay."
32. "Tells Objections to Fort Forrest as Camp's Name."
33. "Granddaughter of Gen. Forrest Spoke on Radio."
34. Tucker, "Tullahoma Plans Expansion."
35. Pyle, *Historic Tullahoma*.
36. "Northern Field, at Tullahoma, Named for Tennessee Air Hero."

37. "Air Training Work Began Year Ago."
38. "Northern Field Bombing Range in Operation."
39. Von Messling and Lynch, "Huddleston."
40. Mr. and Mrs. Dunn, transcript of oral history conducted in 1993, E-33 in Granville, Tennessee, audiocassette, Motlow State Community College.
41. "Federal Officials Study Tullahoma's Housing Problems."
42. "Contract Let for Tullahoma Housing Units."
43. "Federal Officials Study Tullahoma's Housing Problems."
44. Baulch, "Army Pushes Food Clean-Up."
45. Joanne Roberson, unpublished face-to-face interview with Dr. Elizabeth Taylor at South Jackson Civic Center, October 17, 2018.
46. Tucker, "Tullahoma Plans Expansion."
47. "WWII, Camp Forrest Catapulted Tullahoma," *Tullahoma News*, July 17, 2002.
48. Shirley, "Work at Camp Peay."
49. Baulch, "Camp Building Crew."
50. Eddie Sharbur, transcript of oral history conducted in 1993, E-26, in Tullahoma, Tennessee, audiocassette, Motlow State Community College.
51. Seth Bobby Sharbur, transcript of oral history conducted in 1993, E-27, in Tullahoma, Tennessee, audiocassette, Motlow State Community College.
52. Fitts, "At 80, Retirement Isn't in His Vocabulary."
53. Myrtle Pearsol, transcript of oral history conducted in 1993, E-36, in Tullahoma, Tennessee, audiocassette, Motlow State Community College.
54. Baulch, "Telephone Setup at Camp Forrest."
55. Manda Limbaugh, transcript of oral history conducted in 1993, E-48, in Tullahoma, Tennessee, audiocassette, Motlow State Community College.
56. Frank Grant, transcript of oral history conducted in 1993, B-1, in Tullahoma, Tennessee, audiocassette, Motlow State Community College.
57. Mrs. Melvin (Eva Jean) Hindman, transcript of oral history conducted in 1993, E-19, in Tullahoma, Tennessee, audiocassette, Motlow State Community College.
58. Dewey Smith, transcript of oral history conducted in 1993, T-49, in Tullahoma, Tennessee, audiocassette, Motlow State Community College.
59. Dominique, "Attack Will Go On."
60. Clennie Huddleston, transcript of oral history conducted in 1993, E-49, in Tullahoma, Tennessee, audiocassette, Motlow State Community College.
61. "Soldiers Eat Candy Poisoned with Glass."

62. Edna Conway, transcript of oral history conducted in 1993, E-53, in Tullahoma, Tennessee, audiocassette, Motlow State Community College.
63. Joe Getsay, transcript of oral history conducted in 1993, B-5, in Tullahoma, Tennessee, audiocassette, Motlow State Community College.
64. James Pickett, transcript of oral history conducted in 1993, E-51, in Tullahoma, Tennessee, audiocassette, Motlow State Community College.
65. Paul and Marie Boswell, transcript of oral history conducted in 1993, E-42, in Tullahoma, Tennessee, audiocassette, Motlow State Community College.
66. Gowran, "Illinois Troops Train."
67. Russell and Ruby Kelly, transcript of oral history conducted in 1993, E-20, in Tullahoma, Tennessee, audiocassette, Motlow State Community College.
68. Melvin and Eva Jean Hindman, transcript of oral history conducted in 1993, E-19, in Tullahoma, Tennessee, audiocassette, Motlow State Community College.
69. Von Messling, "Cousins Remember Tullahoman Shares."
70. Orala Lelcthy, transcript of oral history conducted in 1993, E-52, in Tullahoma, Tennessee, audiocassette, Motlow State Community College.
71. Von Messling, "Teen Beings Dairy Career."
72. "Recent Librarian Appointments to Army and Navy Post," *ALA Bulletin* 35, no. 6 (June 1941).
73. "Rules Help Men in Learning to Become Soldiers," *Dispatch*, July 11, 1941.
74. "Elaborate Opening Is Planned for Officers' Club at Forrest."
75. "Benefit Opens Camp Forrest Officers' Club."
76. "Quartermaster Work Explained."
77. "Soldiers Hire Taxi for 1,200-Mile Trip."
78. Otis Price, transcript of oral history conducted in 1993, E-34, in Tullahoma, Tennessee, audiocassette, Motlow State Community College.
79. Lloyd McMohan Sr., transcript of oral history conducted in 1993, E-46, in Tullahoma, Tennessee, audiocassette, Motlow State Community College.
80. William B. Brasier letter to Dr. Elizabeth Taylor, May 25, 2017, and July 30, 2018.
81. Baulch, "City of Thirty Thousand."
82. Hindman, transcript of oral history conducted in 1993, E-19, in Tullahoma, Tennessee, audiocassette, Motlow State Community College.

83. Lillian Milburn and Margaret Anderson, transcript of oral history conducted in 1993, E-35, in Tullahoma, Tennessee, audiocassette, Motlow State Community College.

84. Collins and Unfried, *United States Air Force Research Laboratory Report*.

85. Mary Alice McAdams McKisset, transcript of oral history conducted in 1993, B-7, in Tullahoma, Tennessee, audiocassette, Motlow State Community College.

86. Eileen Reeser Harkins, transcript of oral history conducted in 1993, T-8, in Tullahoma, Tennessee, audiocassette, Motlow State Community College.

87. Baulch, "Mosquitoes One of the Worst Enemies."

88. Harkins, transcript of oral history.

89. Dorothy Couch Watson, unpublished face-to-face interview by Dr. Elizabeth Taylor at The Bookshelf, Northgate Mall, June 16, 2017.

90. Judy Jenkins, unpublished face-to-face interview conducted October 16, 2018, at South Jackson Civic Center, Tullahoma, Tennessee.

91. Kenneth and Linda Cunningham, unpublished face-to-face interview conducted October 17, 2018, at South Jackson Civic Center.

92. "Forrest Hospital Patients Like 'Something for Nothing Shops'."

93. Lipscomb, "'Boom' Days of Construction Over."

94. "Army Camp Far Behind Schedule."

95. Tucker, "Tullahoma Plans Expansion."

96. Baulch, "Prostitutes in Automobiles."

97. "Social Disease Spread Low at Camp Forrest."

98. Burns, Sergio and Bennette, "Somewhere in Tennessee."

99. "Camp Forrest Area Barred to Prostitutes."

100. "Camp Carpenter Fatally Beaten."

101. "German Alien Nabbed by FBI."

102. Orala Lelchty, transcript of oral history conducted in 1993, E-52, in Tullahoma, Tennessee, audiocassette, Motlow State Community College.

103. Mr. Boyd, transcript of oral history conducted in 1993, T-66, in Tullahoma, Tennessee, audiocassette, Motlow State Community College.

104. "Nazi POWs Grow Fruit, Vegetables," *Knoxville Journal*, April 8, 1945.

105. Jean Jones, unpublished face-to-face interview by Dr. Elizabeth Taylor at Northgate Mall, June 28, 2016.

106. Louis Pugh, transcript of oral history conducted in 2008 by Jacob Worthington for World History Major Semester Project, http://0374e15. netsolhost.com/email_call/jacob/semester_project.htm.

Chapter 3

107. "Seven Teachers Named."
108. "Era Saw First High School."
109. Johnny Majors, unpublished phone interview by Dr. Elizabeth Taylor August 28, 2016.
110. Lane, "Friendship Started during World War II."
111. Watson, "Daddy Billy Never Knew a Stranger."
112. Dudley Tipps, unpublished face-to-face interview with Dr. Elizabeth Taylor, South Jackson Civic Center, October 17, 2018.
113. Falk, "Child Labor in Southern Defense Areas."
114. Jeannette Holder, unpublished face-to-face interview with Dr. Elizabeth Taylor, at her home, October 16, 2017.
115. Robert Smith Sanders and Patricia Pelot Sanders, transcript of oral history conducted in 2000, MT2000.030, Albert Gore Research Center.
116. "Two New Paralysis Cases in Camp Forrest District," *Chicago Tribune*, August 8, 1941.
117. Lynda Stone Phillips, unpublished face-to-face and email interview with Dr. Elizabeth Taylor at former Red Cross building on South Jackson Street on February 28, 2019.
118. Alberta Parks, unpublished telephone interview with Dr. Elizabeth Taylor, June 12, 2017.
119. James Shubert, transcript of oral history conducted in 2002, MT2002.114, Albert Gore Research Center.
120. James Elkins, transcript of oral history conducted in 2002, MT085_Elkins, Albert Gore Research Center.
121. Robert Smith Sanders and Patricia Pelot Sanders, transcript of oral history conducted in 2000, MT2000.030, Albert Gore Research Center.

Chapter 4

122. Johnson, "One Man's Opinion."
123. "Fisk Singers' Concert Monday."
124. "Soldiers at Camp Forrest to Learn Meaning of 'Southern Hospitality'."
125. "Camp Forrest Christmas Eve Party Arranged."
126. Gray, unpublished interview at Taylor home.
127. "Mother's Day Armed Forces through U.S. United to Honor Mothers Near and Far Away," *Life*, May 25, 1942.

128. Mosley, "Tullahoma Was Already in a Military State."

129. Tunc, "Casablanca."

130. Altum, "Life a Millennium Ago."

131. Sergeant Robert Cook, letter home to wife Helen in Pennsylvania, February 1943.

Chapter 5

132. World War II Honor List of Dead and Missing for the State of Tennessee, War Department, June 1946, NARA, https://www.archives.gov/research/military/ww2/army-casualties/tennessee.html.

133. "Movement of Troops," *Railway Age* 115, issue 21. Simmons-Boardman, Bristol, Connecticut.

134. Long, "One Man's Journey."

135. Paul and Marie Boswell, transcript of oral history conducted in 1993, E-42, in Tullahoma, Tennessee, audiocassette, Motlow State Community College, Tullahoma, Tennessee.

136. Joanne Roberson, unpublished face-to-face interview with Dr. Elizabeth Taylor at South Jackson Civic Center, October 17, 2018.

137. "Shinnying Up Poles Not as Easy as It Looks."

138. Chuck and Hannah Tyler, transcript of oral history conducted in 1993, B-2, in Tullahoma, Tennessee, audiocassette, Motlow State Community College.

139. Cope, who went by the nickname of "Buddy," served in the army until his discharge in October 1945. After the war, he worked for South Central Bell for more than thirty-five years. He died in 1986. "General Forrest among Trainees at Camp Forrest," *Chattanooga Times*, February 3, 1986.

140. Gowran, "Illinois Troops Will Find Camp Morass of Mud."

141. Pavey, transcript of oral history.

142. "Father, 44 and Son, 18, Go Together."

143. Tom Jennings, transcript of oral history conducted in 1993, T-64, in Tullahoma, Tennessee, audiocassette, Motlow State Community College.

144. "Camp Forrest Food Bill Is $750,000."

145. "Mud or Dust Fate of Guard Troops."

146. "Denies Camp Forrest Conditions Unhealthy."

147. Allen Wesley Kirby Collection (AFC/2001/001/69033), Veterans History Project, American Folklife Center, Library of Congress.

148. "26,000 Overshoes Ordered to Beat 'General Mud' at Camp Forrest,

149. "For $6.38 They Better $640 Army Gun Sight."

150. Brooks, "Morale Sags at Camp Forrest."

151. Ibid.

152. James G. Thompson. Letter to the Editor, *Pittsburgh Courier*, originally published January 31, 1942, reprinted April 11, 1942, pg. 5.

153. Dorothy M. Miller interview transcript of oral history 2001, Women Veterans Historical Project, University of North Carolina at Greensboro.

154. Women of the 6888th Central Postal Directory Battalion. Accessed July 3, 2018. https://www.womenofthe6888th.org.

155. Hindman, transcript of oral history.

156. William Goddard, transcript of oral history conducted in 1993, T-54, in Tullahoma, Tennessee, audiocassette, Motlow State Community College.

157. Reeves, "Soldier's Story."

158. Payne, "Soldier's Story."

Chapter 6

159. Glenn and Mary Ruth Flippo, unpublished face-to-face interview by Dr. Elizabeth Taylor at South Jackson Civic Center, October 17, 2018.

160. "Teach Blackout Typing," *Bradford (PA) Evening Star* and *Bradford (PA) Daily Record*, May 3, 1941.

161. Von Messling and Lynch, "World War II, Camp Forrest Changed Young Girl Forever."

162. Ibid., "Teenager Greatly Impacted."

163. Ibid., "Wartime Tullahoma Stubblefields Share Wartime Experiences."

164. James Shubert, transcript of oral history conducted in 2002, MT114_Shubert, Albert Gore Research Center.

165. Allen, Templin and Price, *History of First Baptist Church*.

166. John Reese, unpublished phone interview with Dr. Elizabeth Taylor, October 17, 2017.

167. Mr. McKelvey, transcript of oral history conducted in 1993, P-6 in Tullahoma, Tennessee, audiocassette, Motlow State Community College, Tullahoma, Tennessee.

168. Robert Armstrong, unpublished phone interview with Dr. Elizabeth Taylor, August 2016.

169. Judy Turchin, unpublished phone interview with Dr. Elizabeth Taylor, 2018.

Chapter 7

170. Kramer, *Nazi Prisoners of War.*
171. "Withdraws Charges That POWs Are Being Given Too Much Meat."
172. "No Pampering of PW's at Sheboygan Camp."
173. "Nazi Prisoners to Lose Fresh Meat and Fish."
174. "Camp Forrest Status Undergoes Changes."
175. Kramer, *Nazi Prisoners of War.*
176. Kupsky, "'To Win Our War'."
177. "Prisoners of War Weave Nets for American Forces," *Kingsport News*, March 13, 1945.
178. "18 P.O.W.s Still Are at Large."
179. Hindman, transcript of oral history conducted in 1993, E-19, in Tullahoma, Tennessee, audiocassette, Motlow State Community College.
180. Curtis Cobb, transcript of oral history conducted in 1993, P-3, in Tullahoma, Tennessee, audiocassette, Motlow State Community College, Tullahoma, Tennessee.
181. Justice, "Camp Forrest Research."
182. Charlie and Elizabeth Hensley, unpublished face-to-face interview, The Bookshelf, Northgate Mall, Tullahoma, Tennessee, June 24, 2016
183. Von Messling. "Teen Begins Dairy Career during WWII."
184. Lynn Tolley, unpublished face-to-face interview, The Bookshelf, Northgate Mall, Tullahoma, Tennessee, June 24, 2016.
185. A.L. Bradley, transcript of oral history conducted in 1993, P-4, in Tullahoma, Tennessee, audiocassette, Motlow State Community College.

Chapter 8

186. Barton, "Old Camp Forrest Chapel Building."
187. Barton, "Cowan Minister Brings 'Hope.'"
188. "Manchester Times, Tullahoma News Record Camp Forrest History."
189. "Stewart Asks Forrest as Permanent Post."
190. Pyle, *Historic Tullahoma.*
191. "Housing Release Expected Soon."
192. Beline, "Spunky Erma Duckworth Turns 93."
193. Golden Anniversary of Arnold Engineering Development Center, *Tullahoma News Guardian.*
194. Spinney, *World War II in Nashville.*

195. Candy Couch, unpublished face-to-face interview with Dr. Elizabeth Taylor, Couch's, 117 NW Atlantic Street, Tullahoma, Tennessee, 37388, October 26, 2017.
196. *Historic Tullahoma*, '86 Homecoming Book Committee. Tullahoma, Tennessee, 1986.

BIBLIOGRAPHY

Afro-American. "Says Camp Forrest Command Confines WACs to Kitchen." December 25, 1943.

Allen, Tommy, Eleanor Templin and Betty Price. *A History of First Baptist Church Tullahoma, Tennessee 1853 to 2006*. Tullahoma, TN: Triple Jubilee Celebration, 2006. September 2006. Triple Jubilee Celebration.

Alton Evening Telegraph. "Camp Forrest Ready for Soldiers from Four States." March 3, 1941.

Altum, Greg. "Life a Millennium Ago." *Tullahoma News*, January 1, 2000.

"At Both Ends." *Time* 41, no. 5 (February 1943): 61–62.

Atlanta Constitution. "Camp Forrest Continues, War Department Says." February 24, 1944, 10.

Atlanta Daily World. "Camps Can't Bar Negro Newspapers." July 5, 1941, 1.

———. "Charge White Paratroopers Annoying Colored WACs." August 9, 1944, 1.

———. "For $6.38 They Better $640 Army Gun Sight." July 5, 1941, 1.

Austin American. "Camp Forrest." March 22, 1941.

Barton, Tina. "Old Camp Forrest Chapel Building Proves Just How Much, How Far the Spirit Can Move." *Tullahoma News*, February 1, 1998.

———. "Cowan Minister Brings 'Hope' to Old Camp Forrest Chapel." *Tullahoma News*, April 26, 1998.

Baulch, Jerry T. "Army Pushes Food Clean-Up." *Tennessean*, April 9, 1941.

———. "Camp Building Crew Now Down to 2,287 Workers but There's Shortage of Nurses, Bakers, and Laundry Workers." *Jackson Sun*, March 20, 1941.

———. "City of Thirty Thousand and No Washwoman: Single Laundry Takes Care of Camp Forrest Clothes." *Jackson Sun*, April 27, 1941.

———. "Mosquitoes One of the Worst Enemies for U.S. Soldiers." *Kingsport Times*, May 28, 1941.

———. "Prostitutes in Automobiles at Camp Forrest." *Jackson Sun*, March 26, 1941.

———. "Telephone Setup at Camp Forrest Taxed by Army." *Kingsport Times*, March 11, 1941.

Beline, Tamara. "A Spunky Erma Duckworth Turns 93." *Tullahoma News*, June 8, 2001.

Billinger, Robert D., Jr. *Nazi POWS in the Tar Heel State*. Gainesville: University Press of Florida, 2008.

Bradley, Michael. "Reveille to Taps: Camp Forrest, TN, 1940–1946." Unpublished manuscript. Motlow State Community College Library, Tullahoma, Tennessee.

Brasier, William B. Letter to Dr. Elizabeth Taylor, May 25, 2017, and July 30, 2018.

Brooks, Deton, Jr. "Morale Sags at Camp Forrest as Jim Crow Rules." In *Reporting World War II: Part One American Journalism 1938–1944*, 662–64. New York: Library of America, 1995.

Burnham, Margaret. "Soldiers and Buses: All Aboard." *Race and Justice* 5, no. 2 (2015): 91–113.

Burns, G. Frank, Kelly Sergio and Rex Bennette. "Somewhere in Tennessee, The Cumberland in Wartime, 1940–1947." In *Rural Life and Culture in the Upper Cumberland*, edited by Michael E. Birdwell and W. Calvin Dickinson. Lexington: University Press of Kentucky, 2004.

Chattanooga News-Free Press. "Northern Field, at Tullahoma, Named for Tennessee Air Hero." April 6, 1943.

Chicago Tribune. "Illinois Troops Will Find Camp Morass of Mud." March 11, 1941.

———. "Tells Objections to Fort Forrest as Camp's Name." November 27, 1940.

Collins, M. Thomas, and Karen Unfried. *United States Air Force Research Laboratory Report of Investigation: The Presence of Biological and Chemical Warfare Material at AFMC Bases within the United States*. Wright-Patterson AFB, OH: Simulation Technologies, June 2000.

Cook, Sergeant Robert. Letter home to wife, Helen, in Pennsylvania. February 1943.

Cumberland Evening Times. "Soldiers Hire Taxi for 1,200-Mile Trip." October 15, 1941.

Curlee, Lane (mayor). *History of Tullahoma*. "Tullahoma Time-Table Taking Effect 1852 on the Highland Rim, Coffee County, Tennessee." *The Dixie Highway* 25 (2014–15). Official publication of the Historic Preservation Society of Tullahoma.

Daily News-Journal. "Benefit Opens Camp Forrest Officers' Club." January 20, 1942.

———. "Denies Camp Forrest Conditions Unhealthy." July 10, 1941.

———. "Northern Field Bombing Range in Operation." December 10, 1943.

———. "Soldiers at Camp Forrest to Learn Meaning of 'Southern Hospitality.'" March 11, 1941.

Decatur Daily Review. "Social Disease Spread Low at Camp Forrest." November 25, 1941.

———. "Yule Spirit to Be Present in Camp Forrest." December 22, 1941.

Dement, Rebekah. "The Phenomenon of Five Thousand Soldiers Milling Around One Business Block: World War II and Tullahoma, Tennessee." *Tennessee Historical Quarterly* 68, no. 3 (Fall 2009).

Dispatch (Moline, IL). "Army Camp Far Behind Schedule." January 11, 1941.

Dixon Evening Telegraph. "Federal Officials Study Tullahoma's Housing Problems." April 30, 1941.

Dominique, Dean James. "The Attack Will Go On: The 317th Infantry Regiment in World War II." Master's thesis. Louisiana State University and Agricultural and Mechanical College, 2003.

Falk, Myron. "Child Labor in Southern Defense Areas." *Social Science Review* 16, no. 3 (September 1, 1942): 436–45.

Fitts, Imogene. "At 80, Retirement Isn't in His Vocabulary." *Tullahoma News*, July 26, 2002.

Gowran, Clay. "Illinois Troops Train with Few Up to Date Arms." *Chicago Tribune*, March 22, 1941.

———. "Illinois Troops Will Find Camp Morass of Mud." *Chicago Tribune*, March 11, 1941.

Gray, Alan. Unpublished face-to-face interview at Taylor home on October 18, 2019, and Glenn Miller in World War II. https://glennmiller.org/glenn-miller-history/glenn-miller-in-wwii.

Heisler, Barbara Schmitter. *From German Prisoners of War to American Citizen: A Social History with 35 Interviews*. Jefferson, NC: McFarland and Company, 2013.

Historic Tullahoma. '86 Homecoming Book Committee. Tullahoma, Tennessee, 1986.

Hoyer, Raymond. "The Soldier Town." *Journal of Educational Sociology* 15, no. 8 (April 1942): 486–97.

Jackson Sun. "Camp Forrest Status Undergoes Changes." December 12, 1944

———. "Granddaughter of Gen. Forrest Spoke on Radio." July 1, 1941.

———. "Shinnying Up Poles Not as Easy as It Looks." May 21, 1941.

———. "Withdraws Charges That POWs Are Being Given Too Much Meat." May 10, 1945.

Jeffries, John W. *Wartime America: The World War II Homefront.* Chicago: Ivan R. Dee, 1996.

Johnson, Raymond. "One Man's Opinion: Camp Forrest Launches Vast Athletic Program in New Plant." *Tennessean,* January 11, 1942.

Josephson, Judith Pinkerton. *Growing Up in World War II: 1941 to 1945.* Minneapolis, MN: Lerner Publications, 2003.

Justice, Brian. "Camp Forrest Research Reveals Little Known Facts on War Prisoner's Fate." *Tullahoma News,* July 30, 1995.

Kingsport Times. "Elaborate Opening Is Planned for Officers' Club at Forrest," November 2, 1941.

———. "General Forrest among Trainees at Camp Forrest." February 23, 1941.

———. "Mud or Dust Fate of Guard Troops." March 21, 1941.

———. "Prisoners of War Weave Nets for American Forces." March 13, 1945.

Kramer, Arnold. *Nazi Prisoners of War in America.* Lanham, MD: Scarborough House, 1996.

Kupsky, Gregory. "'To Win Our War with Butter and Beefsteaks.' Camp Crossville and the Treatment of Axis Prisoners of War." Traces, We Bring History to Life. Accessed September 5, 2017. http://www.traces. org/2003conference.gkupsky.html.

Kyvig, David E. *Daily Life in the United States 1920–1940 How Americans Lived Through the Roaring Twenties and the Great Depression.* Chicago: Ivan R. Dee, 2004.

Lane, Elizabeth. "Friendship Started during World War II Still Going Strong Over 60 Years Later." *Tullahoma News,* July 28, 2006.

Lawrence Daily-Journal-World. "Soldiers Like Lectures on War Situation; First Course Completed." April 9, 1942, 1.

Leaf-Chronicle. "Camp Peay Has Lumber Shortages." December 10, 1940.

————. "Quartermaster Work Explained." January 24, 1942.

Lipscomb, John. "'Boom' Days of Construction Over, Tullahoma with Additional Police, Awaits Army Influx." *Tennessean*, February 21, 1941.

Long, Robert. "One Man's Journey: Local Soldier Eyewitness to History." *Manchester Times*, September 18, 1996.

Manchester Times. "Manchester Times, Tullahoma News Record Camp Forrest History." August 13, 2014.

Messenger-Inquirer. "General Ben Lear Sounds Warning: Declares American Losses Would Be 'Overwhelming' If US Enters War." December 2, 1941.

Miller, Dorothy M. Interview, transcript of oral history. Women Veterans Historical Project, University of North Carolina at Greensboro, 2001.

Mosely, Brian. "Tullahoma Was Already in a Military State of Mind." *Tullahoma News*, December 7, 2001.

"Movement of Troops." *Railway Age* 115, no. 21 (November 21, 1943): 832–34.

Northcutt, Peggy. "Blacks an Integral Part of City's WWII Growth." *Tullahoma News*, October 2, 2002.

Northernaire. "Air Training Work Began Year Ago." July 3, 1943.

Palm Beach Post. "War Department Lets Construction Contracts." October 8, 1940.

Pantagraph. "Camp Forrest Area Barred to Prostitutes." May 21, 1942.

Payne, Weldon. "A Soldier's Story: Les Clifton Recalls Horrors of WWII." *Tullahoma News Guardian*, February 2010.

Cook, Corporal Robert E. Division Headquarters Co. APO #80, Eightieth Division. To: Mrs. Robert E. Cook, R.D. #1, Box 203, Derry, PA Sunday Morning February 14, 1943, February 10, 1943, and March 12, 1943.

Personnel Correspondence: From Sergeant Luther E. Meek, Thirtieth Infantry Company I, Camp Forrest, Tennessee, to Miss Sylvia Davis, 1222 East Third Street, Centralia, Illinois, February 25, 1942.

Pyle, Paul. *Historic Tullahoma*. Self-published, 2002.

"Recent Librarian Appointments to Army and Navy Post." *ALA Bulletin* 35, no. 6 (June 1941).

Reeves, Mary. "A Soldier's Story: World War II Veteran Marion Bell Tells of Life and Death in a German POW Camp." *Tullahoma News*, October 5, 1997.

Ross, Powell. "Boom-Dazed Tullahoma Awakes to Reality of Expansion as Workers Start Spending Pay Amounting to $175,000." *Tennessean*, October 27, 1940.

Salem News. "For $6.38 They Better $640 Army Gun Sight." June 28, 1941.

Sheboygan Press. "No Pampering of PW's at Sheboygan Camp: A Strict Routine Is Followed Daily." July 21, 1945.

Shirley, Everett. "Work at Camp Peay, Despite Seeming Confusion, Is Whipping Up Army Home." *Tennessean*, November 17, 1940.

Spinney, Robert. *World War II in Nashville: Transformation of the Homefront.* Knoxville: University of Tennessee Press, 1998.

Stanaland, Dlorice. Transcript of oral history conducted in 2008 by Jacob Worthington for World History Major Semester Project. http://0374e15. netsolhost.com/email_call/jacob/semester_project.htm.

St. Louis Star and Times. "18 P.O.W.s Still Are at Large." February 26, 1948.

Tennessean. "Camp Carpenter Fatally Beaten." February 13, 1941.

———. "Camp Forrest Christmas Eve Party Arranged." December 22, 1943.

———. "Camp Forrest Food Bill Is $750,000." July 27, 1941.

———. "Contract Let for Tullahoma Housing Units." December 23, 1942.

———. "Father, 44 and Son, 18, Go Together." September 29, 1942.

———. "Fisk Singers' Concert Monday." April 26, 1942.

———. "Forrest Hospital Patients Like 'Something for Nothing Shops.'" October 15, 1944.

———. "Gen. Forrest Honored by War Body in Renaming Camp Peay." January 25, 1941.

———. "German Alien Nabbed by FBI: Held at Camp Forrest; Italian Also Picked Up and Kept in Custody." December 14, 1941.

———. "Housing Release Expected Soon." October 31, 1946.

———. "Nazi Prisoners to Lose Fresh Meat and Fish." March 25, 1945.

———. "Seven Teachers Named." January 20, 1942.

———. "Soldiers Eat Candy Poisoned with Glass." February 17, 1918.

———. "'Speculation' Camp Threat, Says Frazier." October 9, 1940.

———. "Stewart Asks Forrest as Permanent Post." March 14, 1946.

———. "26,000 Overshoes Ordered to Beat 'General Mud' at Camp Forrest." March 11, 1941.

———. "Wage Rate Set at Camp Peay." November 24, 1940.

Thompson, James G. Letter to the editor. *Pittsburgh Courier*, originally published January 31, 1942, reprinted April 11, 1942, 5.

Tucker, Randolph. "Tullahoma Plans Expansion to 7 Times Present Size." *Tennessean*, October 13, 1940.

Tullahoma News. "Camp Construction Stirred Economy." October 2, 2002, 37.

———. "Era Saw First High School, Junior High School in City." October 2, 2002.

———. "National Guard's Camp Peay Became Army's Camp Forrest." October 2, 2002.

Tullahoma News Guardian. Golden Anniversary of Arnold Engineering Development Center. Lakeway, 2001.

Tunc, Tanfer Emin. "Casablanca: The Romance of Propaganda." *Bright Lights Film Journal*. Accessed November 3, 2018. www.BrightLights film. com.

Von Messling, Brigitta. "Cousins Remember Tullahoman Shares World War II Memories of Milk Delivery during Camp Forrest Days." *Tullahoma News*, December 5, 1999.

———. "Teen Beings Dairy Career during WWII." *Tullahoma News*, December 5, 1999.

Von Messling, Brigitta, and Kendall Lynch. "Huddleston: Flour Bomb, Training, Visiting Hangouts." *Tullahoma News*, January 1, 2000.

———. "Teenager Greatly Impacted by World War II Era Events." *Manchester Times*, January 1, 2000.

———. "Wartime Tullahoma Stubblefields Share Wartime Experiences That Brought Trials and Tribulation to Area." *Tullahoma News*, January 9, 2000.

———. "World War II, Camp Forrest Changed Young Girl Forever." *Tullahoma News Guardian*, January 1, 2000.

Watson, Dot. "Daddy Billy Never Knew a Stranger." *Tullahoma News Guardian*, May 20, 2018.

Weatherford, Doris. *American Women During World War II—An Encyclopedia*. New York: Routledge, 2010.

Whitman, Sylvia. *Children of the World War II Home Front*. Minneapolis, MN: Carolrhoda Books, 2001.

Women of the 6888th Central Postal Directory Battalion. Accessed July 3, 2018. https://www.womenofthe6888th.org.

World War II Honor List of Dead and Missing for the State of Tennessee, War Department, June 1946, NARA. https://www.archives.gov/research/military/ww2/army-casualties/tennessee.html.

Yarbrough, Willard. "Italians and Germans Have Easy Life in US Prison Camps." *Palm Beach Post-Times*, June 22, 1943.

INDEX

A

African American 32, 33, 36, 80, 89, 109, 110, 112, 113, 114
Arnold Engineering Development Complex (AEDC) 17, 18, 151, 153

C

children 17, 25, 27, 74, 76, 79, 80, 81, 83, 85, 86, 124, 125
construction 9, 10, 11, 14, 22, 25, 31, 34, 35, 36, 37, 39, 40, 43, 44, 45, 47, 48, 53, 57, 58, 59, 73, 74, 85, 97, 102, 105, 125, 127, 135, 143, 148, 150, 151, 153

D

December 7 20, 21, 78, 155, 161, 169

decommission 150

E

enemy aliens 15

H

housing 10, 16, 36, 43, 44, 52, 73, 76, 131, 132, 137, 148

L

laundry 11, 47, 55, 57, 63, 64, 65, 72, 114, 118, 138, 141
Lear, Lieutenant Ben 28, 156, 169
letter writing 144

M

military induction 95

N

Northern Field 11, 40, 41, 44, 48,
        50, 55, 78, 148, 151, 156,
        157, 166, 167

P

Pearl Harbor 10, 18, 19, 20, 25, 26,
        27, 28, 29, 79, 80, 83, 96
prostitution 74, 129

R

rationing 65, 104, 124, 126, 127
Roosevelt, President Franklin D.
        10, 20, 23, 30, 31, 53, 109,
        113

T

Tennessee maneuvers 102
transportation 61, 95, 113
Truman, President Harry 112, 151

W

WAAC
  WAC 114
war games 117

ABOUT THE AUTHOR

D
r. Elizabeth Taylor has researched the many impacts of Camp Forrest both abroad and on the homefront. She currently maintains the Camp Forrest website (www.CampForrest.com) and welcomes individuals to contact her with stories, comments and photographs. She earned a doctorate in public administration and completed master's level coursework in history and political science.